New American STREAMLINE

BERNARD HARTLEY & PETER VINEY

DEPARTURES

An intensive American English series for beginners
Workbook A
Units 1–40
REVISED BY TIM FALLA

Oxford University Press

Oxford University Press

198 Madison Avenue
New York, NY 10016 USA

Great Clarendon Street
Oxford OX2 6DP England

Oxford New York
Athens Auckland Bangkok Bogota Bombay
Buenos Aires Calcutta Cape Town Dar es Salaam
Delhi Florence Hong Kong Istanbul Karachi
Kuala Lumpur Madras Madrid Melbourne
Mexico City Nairobi Paris Singapore
Taipei Tokyo Toronto Warsaw

and associated companies in
Berlin Ibadan

OXFORD is a trademark of Oxford University Press.

ISBN 0-19-434826-1 (Workbook A)

Based on the original American adaptation by
Flamm/Northam Authors and Publishers Services, Inc.

Editorial Manager: Susan Lanzano
Editor: Ken Mencz
Designer: John Daly/Harry Katz
Senior Art Buyer: Alexandra F. Rockafellar
Production Manager: Abram Hall

Cover illustration by: Pete Kelly

Illustrations and realia by: Daniel Abraham, Ray Alma,
Carlos Castellanos, John Daly, Dee DeLoy, Jenny Dubnau,
Rich Garramone, Sandy Hoffman, Tom Powers, Jeff Shelly,
David Slonim, Anne Stanley, William Waitzman,
Rose Zgodzinski

Printing (last digit) 10 9 8 7 6

Printed in Hong Kong.

TO THE TEACHER

Workbook A of *New American Streamline: Departures* consists
of forty units. Each unit relates directly to the corresponding
unit in the Student Book of *New American Streamline:
Departures*, units 1–40.

The Workbook is an optional component of the series,
designed to provide language summaries and additional
written exercises. It may be used in the following ways:

1. In more extensive courses as additional classroom
   material, providing extra oral practice and written
   reinforcement and consolidation of the basic core
   material in the Student Book.
2. As homework material in more intensive situations.

The Workbook should only be used after full oral practice
of the corresponding unit in the Student Book. The language
summaries provide material for review.

Another workbook is available for units 41–80 of the
Student Book, under the title *Workbook B*.

Bernard Hartley
Peter Viney

Unit 1

Language Summary

I	'm / am	a student.
You	're / are	from the United States.
He / She	's / is	

Am	I	a student?
Are	you	from the United States?
Is	he / she	

Yes,	I am.
	you are.
	he is.
	she is.

No,	I	'm not. / am not.
	you	aren't. / are not.
	he	isn't.
	she	is not.

Where	am	I	from?
	are	you / they	
	is	he / she	

A. Is she from England?
No, she isn't.

B. Is he from Italy?
Yes, he is.

C. ....Canada?
....

D. ....Haiti?
....

E. ....France?
....

F. ....Egypt?
....

G. ....Mexico?
....

H. ....Greece?
....

I. ....Colombia?
....

Exercise 2

Look at Exercise 1. Write questions and answers.

A. *Where's she from?*
   She's from Japan.

B. ....

   ....

C. ....

   ....

D. ....

   ....

E. ....

   ....

F. ....

   ....

G. ....

   ....

H. ....

   ....

I. ....

   ....

Exercise 3

Complete this conversation.

A: Hello.

B: ....

A: I'm Anne Hutchinson.

B: ....

A: Are you a teacher?

B: ....

A: Oh, are you a student?

B: ....

A: Are you from the United States?

B: ....

A: Where are you from?

B: ....

Exercise 4

Complete this conversation.

A: Hello, Jessica!

B: ....

A: Fine, thanks. And you?

B: ....

AMANDA   JESSICA

Unit 2

Language Summary

We	're	American.		Are	we	American?		Yes,	we	are.		No,	we	aren't.
You	are	Japanese.			you				you				you	are not.
They	aren't	Spanish.			they				they				they	
	are not													

Exercise 1

Are they businessmen?
No, they aren't.

Are they businessmen?
Yes, they are.

1. ....tourists?
....

2. ....tourists?
....

3. ....teachers?
....

4. ....teachers?
....

Exercise 2

I/France/French   *I'm from France. I'm French.*

1. We/the U.S./American ....
2. He/Canada/Canadian ....
3. She/Mexico/Mexican ....
4. They/Japan/Japanese ....
5. You/Brazil/Brazilian ....
6. It/Spain/Spanish ....
7. You/Ecuador/Ecuadorian ....
8. They/Switzerland/Swiss ....
9. We/Panama/Panamanian ....
10. He/Indonesia/Indonesian ....
11. We/England/English ....
12. They/China/Chinese ....
13. You/Colombia/Colombian ....

Exercise 3

Complete this conversation.

A: Please sit down.

B: ....

A: Coffee?

B: ....

A: Cream?

B: ....

A: Where are you from?

B: ....

A: Are you here on business?

B: ....

A: Are you on vacation?

B: ....

Exercise 4

five twelve three four
ELEVEN eight
two
nine one seven TEN

1. *one*		7.	
2. *two*		8.	
3.		9.	
4.		10.	
5.		11.	
6.		12.	

Unit 3

Language Summary

This	is	a pen.
That	's	an egg.
	is	

What	's	that?
	is	
	is	it?

It	's	a pen.
	is	an egg.

Is	this	a pen?
	that	an egg?
	it	

Yes, it is.
No, it isn't.

These	are	pens.
Those	aren't	eggs.

What are	these?
	those?
	they?

They	are	pens.
	're	eggs.

Are	these	pens?
	those	eggs?

Yes, they are.
No, they aren't.

Exercise 1

Look:

a – b/c/d/f/g/h/j/k/l/m/n/p/q/r/s/t/v/w/x/y/z
an – a/e/i/o/u

It's a pen.   It's an apple.

.... egg.   .... iron.   .... lemon.   .... chair.

.... glass.   .... cup.   .... orange.   .... key.

.... plate.   .... spoon.   .... umbrella.   .... shelf.

Exercise 2

What are they?
They're forks.

What is it?
It's a spoon.

1. ....
....

2. ....
....

3. ....
....

4. ....
....

5. ....
....

6. ....
....

7. ....
....

8. ....
....

Exercise 3

Look at this:

This is a chair.

That's a chair.

These are chairs.

Those are chairs.

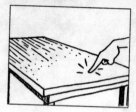

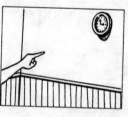

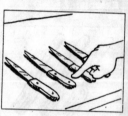

1. ....
2. ....
3. ....
4. ....

Exercise 4

1. ....
2. ....
3. ....
4. ....

Look at this:

/-s/	/-z/	/-ɪz/
book ... books	chair ... chairs	glass ... glasses
cup ... cups	bed ... beds	house ... houses
student ... students	window ... windows	orange ... oranges
fork ... forks	egg ... eggs	bus ... buses
plate ... plates	umbrella ... umbrellas	watch ... watches
truck ... trucks	train ... trains	

Irregular		Note:
foot ... feet	woman ... women	country ... countries
tooth ... teeth	child ... children	**but**
man ... men	knife ... knives	day ... days
	shelf ... shelves	key ... keys

Unit 4

Language Summary

| What's | my
your
his
her | job? | | I'm
You're
He's
She's | a secretary.
a teacher.
a pilot.
a mechanic. | | What are | our
your
their | jobs? | | We're
You're
They're | waiters.
teachers.
flight attendants. |

| Is this your book
Are these your books | here? | | Is that your book
Are those your books | there? |

Exercise 1

A: Excuse me!
B: Yes?
A: Is this your umbrella here?
B: Oh, yes, it is. Thank you.

A: ....
B: ....
A: ....
       keys there?
B: ....
    ....

A: ....
B: ....
A: ....
     suitcase there?
B: ....
    ....

A: ....
B: ....
A: ....
     pens here?
B: ....
    ....

Exercise 2

A: Are you a teacher?
B: No, I'm not.
A: What's your job?
B: I'm a mechanic.

A: .... they waiters?
B: ....
A: ....
B: .... cooks.

A: .... she .... cashier?
B: ....
A: ....
B: .... secretary.

A: .... he .... pilot?
B: ....
A: ....
B: .... police officer.

Exercise 3

your name?/Carlos/Spanish/Mexico

A: What's your name?
B: My name's Carlos.
A: Carlos. That's a Spanish name.
B: Yes, but I'm not Spanish.
A: Oh, where are you from?
B: I'm from Mexico.

Write conversations.

his name?/João/Portuguese/Brazil

her name?/Brigitte/French/Canada

their names?/Kenji and Yoko/ Japanese/the U.S.

1. A: ....
   B: ....
   A: ....
   B: ....
   A: ....
   B: ....

2. A: ....
   B: ....
   A: ....
   B: ....
   A: ....
   B: ....

3. A: ....
   B: ....
   A: ....
   B: ....
   A: ....
   B: ....

Exercise 4

twenty-three eighteen nineteen
fourteen twenty-two seventeen
fifteen thirteen sixteen
twenty-four twenty-one

13. thirteen
14. fourteen
15. ....
16. ....
17. ....
18. ....

19. ....
20. ....
21. ....
22. ....
23. ....
24. ....

Unit 5

Language Summary

I	'm am	cold. hot.	I	'm not am not	cold. hot.	Am	I	young? beautiful? strong?	Yes	I am. it she he	is.
He She It	's is	old. tired. hungry. thirsty.	He She It	isn't is not	old. tired. hungry. thirsty.	Is	he she it		No,	I'm not. it she he	's not. isn't.
You We They	're are		You We They	aren't are not		Are	you we they				

Exercise 1

22 *twenty-two*   14 *fourteen*

12 ....   23 ....   10 ....   13 ....

15 ....   19 ....   4 ....   16 ....

8 ....   11 ....   5 ....   21 ....

Exercise 2

camera/man/book/knife/house

Look at the examples and do the same with: businessman/shelf/pilot/room/mechanic/cook/radio/ suitcase/child/job/woman/dress/watch/student/key/glass.

/-s/	/-z/	/-ɪz/
books	cameras	houses
....	....	....
....	....	....
....	....	....
....	....	....

/-vz/	Irregular
knives	men
....	....
	....
	....

Exercise 3

cold/*hot*   beautiful/*ugly*

big/ ....   thick/ ....   long/ ....

tall/ ....   expensive/ ....   strong/ ....

new/. ....   empty/ ....   young/ ....

thin	cheap
old	full
small	old
weak	short
short	

Exercise 4

He's hot.

She's angry.

Now write sentences with: short/thirsty/hungry/old/tired/late.

1. ....
2. ....
3. ....

1. ....
2. ....
3. ....

Exercise 5

Is it small?

No, it isn't. It's big.

1. Are they weak?

....

2. Is it full?

....

3. Is she young?

....

4. Is it hot?

....

5. Are they long?

....

6. Is he short?

....

7. Is it cheap?

....

8. Is it beautiful?

....

Exercise 6

twenty-six *twenty-seven*

!WENTY !IGHT

25. *twenty-five*
26. ....
27. ....
28. ....
29. ....

Exercise 7

Are you tall?
Yes, I am or *No, I'm not.*

1. Are you strong?

....

2. Is your teacher tall?

....

3. Is your school big?

....

4. Are you hungry?

....

5. Is your teacher tired?

....

Unit 6

Language Summary

There	's	a stove.
	isn't	an apple.
	are	some cups.
	aren't	any glasses.

Is there a stove?

Are there any cups?

It's	in	the refrigerator.
They're	on	
	under	

Yes, there is./No, there isn't.

Yes, there are./No, there aren't.

Where	is it?
	are they?

in   on   under

Exercise 1

There's a garage.
There are three bedrooms.

Write seven sentences.

1. ....
2. ....
3. ....
4. ....
5. ....
6. ....
7. ....

DOWNSTAIRS

DINING ROOM | KITCHEN
CLOSET
LIVING ROOM | HALL | GARAGE

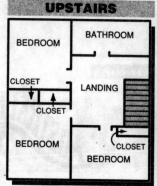

UPSTAIRS

BEDROOM | BATHROOM
CLOSET | LANDING
CLOSET
BEDROOM | CLOSET
BEDROOM

Exercise 2

Write these words on the picture:
pens/chair/lamp/shelf/clock

Exercise 3

lamp   There's a lamp in the office.
VCR   There isn't a VCR in the office.

Write sentences with: desk/table/fax machine/television.

1. ....
2. ....
3. ....
4. ....

CABINET

WORD PROCESSOR

FLOPPY DISKS

BOOKS

TELEPHONE

WASTEPAPER BASKET

DESK

FAX MACHINE

DRAWER

Exercise 4

pens   *There are some pens on the desk.*   Write sentences with: books/floppy disks.

1. ....

2. ....

Exercise 5

books/desk   *There aren't any glasses on the desk.*   Write sentences with: magazines/desk   floppy disks/shelf   pens/cabinet.

cups/cabinet   *There aren't any cups in the cabinet.*

1. ....

2. ....

3. ....

Exercise 6

Where's the telephone?
It's on the desk.

Where are the books?
They're in the cabinet.

1. .... clock?
.... shelf.

2. ....word processor?
.... desk.

3. .... wastepaper basket?
.... desk.

4. .... floppy disks?
.... desk.

5. .... pens?
.... desk.

6. .... lamp?
.... desk.

Exercise 7

Write sentences about your bedroom with:
There's...
There isn't...

There are...
There aren't...

. ....

. ....

. ....

. ....

. ....

6. ....

7. ....

8. ....

9. ....

10. ....

Exercise 8

Look at Exercise 1. Write sentences
about your house or apartment with:
There's ...
There are ...

. ....

. ....

. ....

4. ....

5. ....

6. ....

Unit 7

Could	you	pass the salt?
	I	
	he	
	she	

How much	is...?
	are...?

Exercise 1

salt   *Could you pass the salt, please?*

Write sentences with:
bread / sugar / cream / mustard / pepper / ketchup.

1. ....

2. ....

3. ....

4. ....

5. ....

6. ....

Exercise 2

20. *twenty*

30. ....

40. ....

50. ....

60. ....

70. ....

80. ....

90. ....

twenty   EIGHTY   *forty*   SIXTY
seventy   THIRTY
fifty   ninety

Look at this:

$1.00	one dollar
$2.00	two dollars
$15.00	fifteen dollars
$1.20	a dollar twenty

$3.50	three dollars and fifty cents
$4.87	four eighty-seven

Exercise 3

$1.38   *a dollar thirty-eight*

$6.08   *six dollars and eight cents / six oh-eight*

$1.51 ....

$7.84 ....

$11.17 ....

$3.92 ....

$1.47 ....

$1.10 ....

$10.78 ....

$22.39 ....

$16.06 ....

$12.65 ....

$8.23 ....

$4.80 ....

Exercise 4

How much is this?
Five dollars and forty cents.

How much is that?
One ninety-eight.

1. ....
....

2. ....
....

Exercise 5

15¢ *fifteen cents*

30¢ ....

50¢ ....

95¢ ....

13¢ ....

89¢ ....

60¢ ....

40¢ ....

10¢ ....

75¢ ....

Exercise 6

☎ TELEPHONE NUMBERS

Josh 674-6083
Keiko 276-3991
Mr. & Mrs. Chang 471-4710
Dave & Maria (205) 772-9912
Mike (914) 748-3319

A: *Is Josh in your phone book?*
B: *Yes, he is.*
A: *What's his number?*
B: *674-6083.*

Write conversations about: Keiko,
Mr. and Mrs. Chang, Dave and Maria,
Mike.

1. A: ....

   B: ....

   A: ....

   B: ....

2. A: ....

   B: ....

   A: ....

   B: ....

3. A: ....

   B: ....

   A: ....

   B: ....

4. A: ....

   B: ....

   A: ....

   B: ....

Exercise 7

Complete the conversation.

A: Hi. An orange soda, please.

B: ....?

A: Large, please.

B: ....

A: Thanks. ....?

B: $1.50.

A: Thank you.

B: ....

	Regular	Large
Lemon-Lime Soda	$1.15	$1.50
Orange Soda	$1.15	$1.50
Lemonade	$1.50	$2.50

ORANGE LEMON-LIME LEMONADE

Look at this:

1 pint	=	0.470 liters
1/2 pint	=	0.235 liters
8 pints	=	1 gallon (4 quarts)
1 gallon	=	3.785 liters

Unit 8

Language Summary

Who	is it?		It's	Tom. He's	a doctor.		What color	is it?		It's	yellow.
	's	this?		Mary. She's				are they?		They're	
	is	that?									

It's	Tom's	shirt.
They're		pants.

Exercise 1

Diane Martin

fire fighter
flight attendant
lifeguard
baseball player
soccer player

A. *Who is it?*
It's Diane Martin.
She's a fire fighter.

Harry Hall

Amy Tan

Brian Ross

Hector Perez

B. ....?
....

C: ....?
....

D. ....?
....

E. ....?
....

Exercise 2

Tom/shirt   *It's Tom's shirt.*
Maria/jeans   *They're Maria's jeans.*

1. Mr. Geiger/jacket

....

2. Ellen/skirt

....

3. Mike/shorts

....

4. Mr. Taylor/cap

....

5. Mrs. Martin/blouse

....

6. Nathan/pants

....

7. Natasha/shoes

....

8. Ms. Garcia/dress

....

9. Jimmy/watch

....

10. Mr. Schiff/car

....

11. Erica/T-shirt

....

12. Mrs. Canino/hat

....

INTERNATIONAL SOCCER COLORS

COUNTRY	SHIRT	SHORTS	SOCKS
ENGLAND	WHITE	BLUE	WHITE & BLUE
USA	RED & WHITE	BLUE	WHITE
MEXICO	GREEN	RED	RED & GREEN
URUGUAY	BLUE & WHITE	BLACK	BLUE
BRAZIL	YELLOW & GREEN	GREEN	YELLOW
ITALY	BLUE	WHITE	BLUE & WHITE
GERMANY	WHITE	BLACK	BLACK & WHITE

Brazil   *What color's the shirt? It's yellow and green.*
Germany   *What color are the shorts? They're black.*
England   *What color are the socks? They're white.*
Write sentences about: England/the U.S.A./
Uruguay/Brazil/Italy/Germany/your country.

1. ....
2. ....
3. ....
4. ....
5. ....
6. ....
7. ....

Today my skirt is green. My blouse is white and my jacket is blue. My shoes are brown. Are these colors right on your TV? Is your TV a Mony?

Now write about your clothes.

....
....
....

Now write about your teacher's clothes.

....
....
....

Unit 9

Whose	car is it?		It	's	John's (car).		They	're	Mr. Smith's (sunglasses).
	shoes are they?			is	Mary's (car).			are	

Exercise 1

1. What is it?
   It's a car.
2. Who is it?
   It's Sandra.
3. Whose car is it?
   It's Sandra's.

1. ....

....

2. ....

....

3. ....

....

1. ....

....

2. ....

....

3. ....

....

1. ....

....

2. ....

....

3. ....

....

1. ....

....

2. ....

....

3. ....

....

1. ....

....

2. ....

....

3. ....

....

Exercise 2

William + Melissa

Stacy   Robert

William is Melissa's husband.
William is Stacy's father.
William is Robert's father.

Write three sentences about: Melissa, Stacy, and Robert.

Melissa

1. ....

2. ....

3. ....

Stacy

1. ....

2. ....

3. ....

Robert

1. ....

2. ....

3. ....

Exercise 3

Gloria King's very rich.
She's a movie star.
Gloria's car is Italian.
It's a Ferrari.

Look at the information above.
Now complete this conversation.

A: Hi there.

B: ....   A: Is it your car?

A: Wow! What's that?   B: ....

B: ....   A: Whose car is it?

A: Is it a German car?   B: ....

B: ....   A: Gloria King? Who's she?

A: Where's it from?   B: ....

B: ....

Unit 10

Language Summary

| There | 's some | water in the pitcher. |
| | isn't any | |

Is there any water in the pitcher? | Yes, there is.
| No, there isn't.

How much water is there?   There's a lot.

| There | are some | apples in the refrigerator. |
| | aren't any | |

Are there any apples in the refrigerator? | Yes, there are.
| No, there aren't.

How many apples are there?   There are a lot.

Exercise 1

Write these words in the correct category: rice/honey/
bananas/onions/cheese/tomatoes/mushrooms/lemonade/meat/
oil/hamburgers/peas/eggs/sugar/oranges/salt/milk/lemons.

apples ....
....

water ....
....

Exercise 2

There's some milk.   *There are some apples.*

Write six sentences.

1. .... 4. ....
2. .... 5. ....
3. .... 6. ....

Exercise 3

sugar   *There isn't any sugar.*

tomatoes   *There aren't any tomatoes.*

Write sentences with: oil/eggs/onions/
rice/hamburgers/ice cream.

1. .... 4. ....
2. .... 5. ....
3. .... 6. ....

Exercise 4

Is there any milk? *Yes, there is.*
Is there any water? *No, there isn't.*
Are there any peas? *No, there aren't.*
Are there any grapes? *Yes, there are.*

1. .... eggs? ....
2. .... butter? ....
3. .... oil? ....
4. .... lemons? ....
5. .... cheese? ....
6. .... hamburgers? ....
7. .... grapes? ....
8. .... rice? ....

Exercise 5

How much butter is there?
There's a lot.
How many bananas are there?
There are a lot.

1. .... cheese ....?
....
2. .... apples ....?
....
3. .... milk ....?
....
4. .... lemons ....?
....

Unit 11

Language Summary

I'd like	dessert.		Which	soup	would you like?
I would like	a menu.			vegetables	
	some cheese.			dessert	
	some peas.				

❖ Menu ❖

Appetizers   Price

Side Dishes   Price

Entrees

Desserts

Vegetables

all entrees with a choice of:

Beverages

Sorry, no credit cards accepted.

Now write these words on the menu: Tomato Soup / French Fries / Tea / Filet of Sole / Cola / Apple Pie / Coffee / Tomato Juice / Fried Mushrooms / Peas / Beef Stew / Milk / Baked Potato / Steak / Cauliflower / Carrots / Green Salad / Mushroom Omelette / Roast Chicken / Spinach Salad / Ice Cream / Green Beans / Roast Lamb / Onion Soup.

Write the prices for your country.

Exercise 1

fried mushrooms/$3.70   *How much are the fried mushrooms?*
                         They're three seventy.

filet of sole/$11.50   *How much is the filet of sole?*
                        It's eleven fifty.

Write sentences with: tomato juice/french fries/ice cream/green salad/roast chicken/roast lamb/tea.
Use the prices from your menu.

1. ....

   ....

2. ....

   ....

3. ....

   ....

4. ....

   ....

5. ....

   ....

6. ....

   ....

7. ....

   ....

Exercise 2

menu   *I'd like a menu, please.*   potatoes   *I'd like some potatoes, please.*

Write sentences with: an omelette/peas/orange/vegetables/cup of coffee/glass of cola/carrots/mushrooms.

1. ....

2. ....

3. ....

4. ....

5. ....

6. ....

7. ....

8. ....

Exercise 3

soup   *Which soup would you like?*

Write sentences with: dessert/vegetables/ice cream.

1. ....   2. ....   3. ....

Exercise 4

Complete this conversation.

You: Waiter!

Waiter: Yes, sir?

You: .... menu, please.

Waiter: There you go, sir.

You: .... soup.

Waiter: Chicken soup?

You: .... some roast beef.

Waiter: Yes sir, and which vegetables would you like?

You: ....

Waiter: Certainly, sir. Would you like dressing on your salad?

You: ....

Waiter: Which dressing would you like, sir?

You: ...., please.

Unit 12

Language Summary

Jump!		*Don't*	go up the ladder.	Put	them	on.		Look at	me.
Go right!			sit down.		it				him.
Be careful!			touch.	Take	them	off.			her.
			open the door.		it				it.
				Turn	them	on.			us.
					it	off.			them.
									Chrissy.
									Mr. Carter.

Exercise 1

stay at home   *Stay at home.*
go to work   *Don't go to work.*

Make more sentences.

go to bed

1. ....

take this medicine

2. ....

drink beer

3. ....

drink fruit juice

4. ....

Exercise 2

Turn the lights off.   *Turn them off.*

Put your jacket on.   *Put it on.*

Put your boots on...

Turn the radio on. ....

Take your shoes off. ....

Put your socks on. ....

Put your watch on. ....

Turn the television off. ....

Turn the CD player on. ....

Take your coat off..

Exercise 3

Exercise 4

Look at this:

It's my pen.   *Give it to me.*

It's his book.   *Give it to him.*

It's her key.   *Give it to her.*

They're our pens. ....

It's his hat. ....

They're their magazines. ....

It's his briefcase ....

They're her shoes.   *Give them to her.*

They're our books.   *Give them to us.*

They're their keys.   *Give them to them.*

It's her purse . ...

They're my videos. ....

They're our suitcases. ....

It's their book. ....

Exercise 5

Look at this:

he | him | his

Now complete this chart.

I	....	....
....	us	....
they	....	....
....	....	her
you	....	....

Exercise 6

Look at the picture. Write the instructions.

....

....

....

Unit 13

What make is your car?		It's a Ford.	What kind (of camera)	is	it?	It's a (Nikon).
			What kind (of pens)	are	they?	They're (Parkers).

Exercise 1

What kind is it?
It's a Sony.
It's Japanese.

a Sony TV
Japanese

What kind is it?
It's Chanel.
It's French.

Chanel perfume
French

a Boeing 747
American

Lindt chocolate
Swiss

a fur coat
Russian

a Jaguar
British

1. ....
   ....
   ....

2. ....
   ....

3. ....
   ....

4. ....
   ....

a Philips VCR
Dutch

5. ....
   ....
   ....

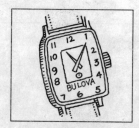

a Bulova watch
American

6. ....
   ....
   ....

Exercise 2

1990   *nineteen ninety*
1959   *nineteen fifty-nine*

You do the same.

1998	1931	1662 ....
1975	1748	1947 ....
1820	1982	1913 ....
1963	1996	1585 ....

Exercise 3

A: *My camera's a Kodak.*
What kind of camera is that?
B: *It's a Pentax.*

Now write conversations.

1. A: .... television ....

................................?

B: ....

2. A: .... CD player ....

................................?

B: ....

3. A: .... car ....

................................?

B: ....

Exercise 4

Christopher/car/Chevrolet
What make is Christopher's car?
It's a Chevrolet.

1. Amanda/Audi

....

....

2. Mr. and Mrs. Patton/Dodge

....

....

Exercise 5

In my room, there's a bed, a lamp, and a desk. There are three shelves, there are some books, and there are two chairs.

Write sentences.

In my bedroom, ...

....

In my house, ...

....

In my kitchen, ...

....

Exercise 6

REVIEW

Read Units 1–12 in the Student Book. Complete these sentences.

Unit 1. His jacket's yellow. He's from .... (6 letters)

Unit 2. Please .... down! (3 letters)

Unit 3. It's an .... (3 letters)

Unit 4. She's a .... (12 letters)

Unit 5. There's a thick .... and a thin .... (4 letters + 4 letters)

Unit 6. There's a small .... under the sink. (5 letters)

Unit 7. Could you .... the salt, please? (4 letters)

Unit 8. Tiffany Gonzalez's .... is pink. (6 letters)

Unit 9. Jessica Montana is Dan's .... (4 letters)

Unit 10. The hamburgers, peas, and pizzas are in the .... (7 letters)

Unit 11. The soup is $2.50. It's .... (6 letters)

Unit 12. Jump! Be very .... ! (7 letters)

Unit 14

Language Summary

I	can	drive.		Can	I	drive?		Yes,	I	can.
You		ski.			you	ski?			you	
He	can't	type.			he	type?		No,	he	can't.
She	cannot	dance.			she	dance?			she	
It		sing.			it	sing?			it	
We		swim.			we	swim?			we	
They		play tennis.			they	play tennis?			they	
		speak French.				speak French?				

Exercise 1

Look at this picture.
I can see a police officer.
I can't see a house.
Write sentences with: truck/bus/car/
taxi/bus stop/pizzeria/bicycle/sofa.

1. ....
2. ....
3. .... 5. .... 7. ....
4. .... 6. .... 8. ....

Exercise 2

I can dance.   *I can't* speak Arabic.
Write sentences.

1. .... cook.   3. .... speak Spanish.   5. .... drive.   7. .... ski.
2. .... play the piano.   4. .... play tennis.   6. .... type.   8. .... swim.

Exercise 3

Can you cook?   *Yes, I can.*
Can you type?   *No, I can't.*

Answer these questions.

1. Can you speak Japanese?...
2. Can you play golf?...
3. Can you drive? ....
4. Can you cook? ....
5. Can you swim?...
6. Can you dance? ....

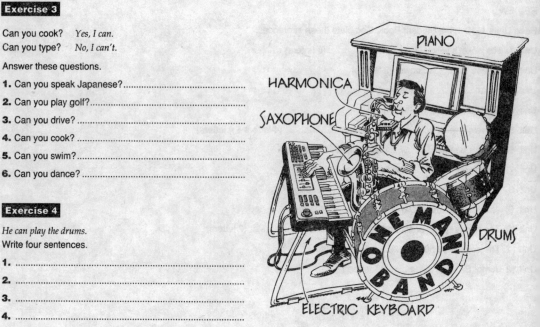

Exercise 4

He can play the drums.
Write four sentences.

1. ....
2. ....
3. ....
4. ....

Unit 15

Language Summary

Would you like	a glass of water?
	coffee or tea?

Exercise 1

A: *Would you like milk or juice?*

B: *Some juice, please.*

A: *How about an orange?*

B: *No, thanks. I'm not hungry.*

Now write conversations.

a cup of coffee/tea   piece of cake   some cola/mineral water sandwich

A: ....

B: ....

A: ....

B: ....

A: ....

B: ....

A: ....

B: ....

Exercise 2

Look at this:

a pair of shoes   a pair of glasses
a pair of socks   a pair of shorts
a pair of pants   a pair of gloves
a pair of tights   a pair of sneakers
a pair of jeans   a pair of boots

A: *I'd like a pair of shoes, please.*
B: *What size are you?*
A: *Seven.*

Write conversations.

A: .... boots ....

B: .... ?

A: ....

A: .... sneakers ....

B: .... ?

A: ....

Exercise 3

A: *These are nice pants!*
B: *Can I try them on?*
A: *This is a nice sweater!*
B: *Can I try it on?*

Write conversations.

1. A: .... dress!

    B: .... ?

2. A: .... shoes!

    B: .... ?

3. A: .... jacket!

    B: .... ?

4. A: .... sneakers!

    B: .... ?

Exercise 4

Complete the conversation.

You: Hi. A frozen yogurt, please.

Counterperson: .... ? Strawberry or vanilla?

You: ....

Counterperson: In a sugar cone or in a cup?

You: In ....

Counterperson: .... That's a dollar ninety-five.

Unit 16

Language Summary

I	have	a car.	Do	I	have	a car?	Yes,	I	do.
You		a house.		you		a house?	No,	you	don't.
We	don't have	a radio.		we		a radio?		we	
They	do not have			they				they	
He	has		Does	he			Yes,	he	does.
She				she			No,	she	doesn't.
It	doesn't have			it				it	
	does not have								

NEW CALYPSO

CENTRAL MOTORS

There are three models:

	Calypso Standard	Calypso Deluxe	Calypso GT Deluxe
RADIO	✗	✓	✓
STEREO CD PLAYER	✗	✗	✓
POWER WINDOWS	✗	✓	✓
SUN ROOF	✗	✗	✓
CLIMATE CONTROL SYSTEM	✗	✗	✓

Exercise 1

Look at the Calypso Standard.   *It doesn't have a radio.*

Write four sentences.

1. ....
2. ....
3. ....
4. ....

Exercise 2

Look at the Calypso GT Deluxe.   *It has a radio.*

Write four sentences.

1. ....
2. ....
3. ....
4. ....

Exercise 3

Look at the Calypso Deluxe.
It has a radio.
It doesn't have a stereo CD player.

Write three sentences.

1. ....
2. ....
3. ....

Exercise 4

A: *Do you have a sister?*
B: *Yes, I do.*
Write questions and answers.

1. **A:** .... brother?
   B: ....

2. **A:** .... VCR?
   B: ....

3. **A:** .... lot of money?
   B: ....

4. **A:** .... CD player?
   B: ....

5. **A:** .... computer?
   B: ....

6. **A:** .... swimming pool?
   B: ....

Unit 17

Language Summary

What	do you	have?
How much	does she	
How many		

Do you have anything to declare?

Exercise 1

100 *one hundred*   200 *two hundred*   300 *three hundred*

400 ....   600 ....   800 ....

500 ....   700 ....   900 ....

Exercise 2

154 *one hundred and fifty-four*   223 ....   896 ....

768 *seven hundred and sixty-eight*   405 ....   349 ....

Exercise 3

How much gold do you have?
How many watches do you have?

Now write questions.

1. .... portable CD players .... ?

2. .... CDs .... ?

3. .... perfume .... ?

4. .... cameras .... ?

5. .... money .... ?

Exercise 4

Look at this:

How much cola do you have?
How many bottles of cola do you have?

Now write sentences.

1. .... gas .... ?

2. .... gallons of gas .... ?

3. .... cheese .... ?

4. .... pounds of cheese .... ?

5. .... coffee .... ?

6. .... pounds of coffee .... ?

7. .... perfume .... ?

8. .... bottles of perfume .... ?

Exercise 5

Complete this conversation.

Customs Officer: .... passport?

Man: Sure. Here it is.

Customs Officer: .... OK. ....
...............................declare?

Man: Yes, I do.

Customs Officer: What .... ?

Man: Some perfume and some CDs.

Customs Officer: .... perfume

...................................?

Man: One bottle.

Customs Officer: .... CDs

...................................?

Man: Three.

Customs Officer: .... watches?

Man: No, I don't.

Customs Officer: That's fine, thank you. Next!

Unit 18

Language Summary

Which	one	's is	mine? yours? his?	The	blue red small	one	's is	mine. yours. his.	I You He	'd would	like	a new car.
	ones	are	hers? ours? theirs? Anne's?		new American	ones	are	hers. ours. theirs. Anne's.	She We They			

Exercise 1

Look at this:

It's my pen. It's mine.
It's your book. It's yours.
It's his watch. It's his.
It's her purse. It's hers.
It's our classroom. It's ours.
It's your car. It's yours.
It's their house. It's theirs.
They're our chairs. They're ours.

1. They're our books. ....

2. It's his knife. ....

3. It's their apartment. ....

4. It's Lee's glass. ....

5. It's our car. ....

6. They're her shoes. ....

7. It's my jacket. ....

8. They're Jasmine's pens..................

Exercise 2

I/car/old/new   *I have an old car, but I'd like a new one.*

1. They/house/small/big

....

2. We/computer/black and white/color

....

3. He/suit/blue/gray

....

4. She/watch/American/Swiss

....

5. You/pen/cheap/expensive

....

Exercise 3

He/small/ones   *Which ones would he like? He'd like the small ones.*

1. They/American/ones

....
....

2. She/new/one

....
....

3. You/green/one

....
....

4. They/cheap/ones

....
....

Exercise 4

Complete this conversation.

A: .... salad?

B: Thanks.

A: .... plate ....

B: That ....

A: Which one?

B: ....

Exercise 5

Complete this conversation.

A: Well, good night and ....
    wonderful evening!

B: Which coat's yours?

A: That ....

B: Which one?

A: .... blue ....

B: Ah, yes. Good night!

A: ....

Unit 19

Language Summary

May	I	borrow your newspaper?		What time is it?	It's	10:00.
Can						4:20.

Exercise 1

Look at this:

1,000 *one thousand*
2,000 *two thousand*
3,000 *three thousand*

4,000 ....

5,000 ....

6,000 ....

7,000 ....

8,000 ....

9,000 ....

10,000 ....

15,000 ....

20,000 ....

21,000 ....

49,000 ....

92,000 ....

Exercise 2

It's three o'clock.

1. .... **2.** .... **3.** .... **4.** .... **5.** ....

....

Exercise 3

It's six-forty.

1. .... **2.** .... **3.** .... **4.** .... **5.** ....

....

Exercise 4

May I borrow your newspaper, please?

1. .... **2.** .... **3.** ....

....

Exercise 5

Complete this conversation.

A: .... your ticket, please?

B: Yes. Here it is.

A: OK. .... ?

B: Yes, one suitcase.

A: Put it right here.

B: ....?

It isn't heavy.

A: No, ...

Language Summary

What	's is	Denver	like?
	are	the people	

Exercise 1

Look at this:

Rd.—Road
Dr.—Drive
Ave.—Avenue
St.—Street
Blvd.—Boulevard
Apt.—Apartment

44101—Zip Code (USA)
K9J 7B8—Postal Code (Canada)

Mr. Robert Middleton
Mrs. Susan Clark or Ms. Susan Clark
Miss Isabel Diaz or Ms. Isabel Diaz

Ms. Jessica King
2014 Cypress Dr.
Spring, TX 77373

Now write these addresses on the envelopes.

Mrs. Peggy Dromgold / 166 East 34th St. / Apt. 601 / New York, NY 10016
Mr. Michael Wilson / 30 Hillsboro Ave. / Toronto, Ontario M5R 1S7 Canada

VIA AIR MAIL

Exercise 2

New York / exciting
What's New York like?
It's exciting.

people / friendly
What are the people like?
They're friendly.

1. the weather / rainy

....

....

2. the buildings / tall

....

....

3. the food / excellent

....

....

4. restaurants / expensive

....

....

Exercise 3

This is Kimberly's first letter to her new pen pal, Carlos.

Now write a letter in English to a pen pal in the United States.

2341 MacArthur Blvd.
Ft. Lauderdale, FL 33344
U.S.A.

August 7

Dear Carlos,
My name's Kimberly Cooper. I'm 18 and I'm single. I'm a secretary. I'm from Fort Lauderdale in Florida. It's a modern town with a lot of tall buildings. It has a population of around 150,000. In the summer it's very hot. There's a long beach, and there are lots of good restaurants and nightclubs.
    Please write to me in Spanish!

Best wishes,
Kimberly

INTERNATIONAL PEN PALS
Write to people in other countries

Unit 21

Language Summary

I	'm
	am
	'm not
	am not
He	's
She	is
It	
	isn't
	is not
We	're
You	are
They	aren't
	are not

working.
sleeping.
eating.
drinking.
sitting.
standing.

Am	I
Is	he
	she
	it
Are	we
	you
	they

working?
sleeping?
eating?
drinking?
sitting?
standing?

Yes,	I	am.
	she	
	he	is.
	it	
	you	
	we	are.
	they	
No,	I'm	not.
	she	isn't.
	he	
	it	's not.
	you	
	we	aren't.

Exercise 1

work *working*
type *typing*
sit *sitting*

1. dance ....

2. cook ....

3. eat ....

4. run ....

5. drink ....

6. sing ....

7. swim ....

8. write ....

Exercise 2

What are they doing?
They're writing.

1. ....
....

2. ....
....

3. ....
....

4. ....
....

5. ....
....

6. ....
....

7. ....
....

8. ....
....

9. ....
....

10. ....
....

11. ....
....

Unit 22

Language Summary

What	's	she	reading?
	is	he	

She	's	reading a book.
He	is	

Who	's	she	talking to ?
	is	he	
	are	you	

She	's	talking to	her	friend.
He	is		his	
I	am		my	

Who's playing football?   David is.
David and Pamela are.

Exercise 1

Michelle's reading.
What's she reading?
She's reading a magazine.

1. ....

....

.... coffee.

2. ....

....

.... fish.

3. ....

....

.... a letter

Exercise 2

Who's reading a magazine?
Michelle is.

Who's drinking coffee?
Steve and Laura are.

1. ....

....

2. ....

....

Exercise 3

He's asking someone.
Who's he asking?

They're watching something.
What are they watching?

1. They're drinking something.

....

2. They're meeting someone.

....

3. She's talking to someone.

....

4. She's cooking something.

....

5. He's reading something.

Exercise 4

talking

watching

meeting

helping

A: Who's Denise talking to?
She's talking to her
boyfriend.

B: Who's talking to her
boyfriend?
Denise is.

1. A: ....

....

B: ....

....

2. A: ....

....

B: ....

....

3. A: ....

....

B: ....

....

Unit 23

Language Summary

Can	you	show	it	to	me?	Can	you	show	me	a camera?
Could		give	them		him?	Could		give	him	some pens?
		bring	one		her?			bring	her	one?
			some		us?				us	some?
					them?				them	

Exercise 1

magazine/Now/$2.50

A: Can I help you?
B: *Yes, I'm looking for a magazine.*
A: What's the title?
B: Now. *Do you have it?*
A: Yes, we do.
B: *How much is it?*
A: $2.50.

CD/Monday Blues/$14.95

A: Can I help you?

B: ....

A: What's the title?

B: ....

A: Yes, we do.

B: ....

A: $14.95.

cassette/Instant English/$19.95

A: ....

B: ....

A: ....

B: ....

A: ....

B: ....

A: ....

Exercise 2

It's a nice camera!
Can you show it to me, please?
They're nice watches!
Can you show them to me, please?

1. It's a nice color TV!

....

2. They're nice pens!

....

3. They're nice clocks!

....

4. It's a nice watch!

....

5. It's a nice CD player!

....

Exercise 3

Send a postcard to me.
Send me a postcard.

1. Bring the check to us.

....

2. Show the pen to her.

....

3. Get some coffee for me.

....

4. Give the book to me.

....

Exercise 4

It's mine!   *Give it to me.*
They're Anne's!   *Give them to her.*

1. It's hers!

....

2. It's theirs!

....

3. They're ours!

....

4. It's David's!

....

5. They're mine!

....

Exercise 5

Complete this conversation.

A: ....some radios, please?

B: Sure. This one's very nice.

A: ....?

B: $229.

A: Oh ....

B: How much can you spend?

A: ....$150.

B: ....$149.95.

A: Good. .... ?

Unit 24

Language Summary

What's	your shirt	made of?	It's	made of	cotton.	It's a	long	dark	blue	nylon	skirt.
What are	your jeans		They're		wool.		short	light	brown	cotton	dress.
					silk.		big		gray	polyester	
					leather.		small		yellow	wool	

He's wearing brown shoes. She's wearing brown shoes, too.
He's a student. She's a student, too.

He isn't a teacher. She isn't a teacher either.

Exercise 1

It's a cotton shirt.
It's a blue shirt.
It's a blue cotton shirt.

She has a long skirt
She has a black skirt.
She has a long black skirt.

1. She's wearing a nylon blouse.
She's wearing a white blouse.

....

2. They have dark blue suits.
They have wool suits.

....

3. They're black shoes.
They're leather shoes.

....

4. It's a green dress.
It's a short dress.

....

5. He's wearing a big sweater.
He's wearing a gray sweater.

....

6. It's a red hat.
It's a small hat.

....

Exercise 2

long/skirt/black/nylon
a long, black nylon skirt

1. dress/cotton/pink/short

....

....

2. leather/brown/shoe/big

....

....

3. wool/blue/sweater/long

....

....

4. gray/blouse/small/cotton

....

....

Exercise 3

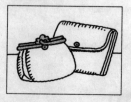   

bags/leather
The bags are made of leather.

shirt/silk
The shirt is made of silk.

sweaters/cotton

1. ....

bottle/glass

2. ....

Exercise 4

1. He can ride a bicycle.

....

2. He has a backpack.

....

3. She's wearing shorts.

....

4. She's riding a bicycle now.

....

He's Canadian.
She's Canadian too.

Exercise 5

Peter's a student.
He isn't rich. *I'm not rich either.*

1. He doesn't have a million dollars.

2. He isn't studying Chinese.

3. He can't speak ten languages.

Unit 25

Exercise 1

on

under

in

inside

outside

between

in front of

behind

Exercise 2

into

out of

up

down

along

across

around

Exercise 3

1. The first elevator is going
....

2. The second elevator is
coming ....

3. The small car is going
.... the parking garage.

4. The big car is coming
.... the parking garage.

5. The cat's ....
the chair.

6. The mouse is
.... the chair.

7. The man's driving the car
.......................the street.

8. The dog's running
.... the street.

9. The man's ....
the tree.

10. The lion's ....
the tree.

11. A lot of people are
.... the stadium.

12. Stephanie is ....
the stadium.

13. Baltimore-Washington
International Airport's
.... the U.S.A.

14. It's .... Washington
and Baltimore.

15. The truck's coming
.... the bend.

Exercise 4

Why's he closing the window?
Because he's cold.

Why can't she buy it?
Because it's very expensive.

Now write answers using: she's married/it's behind the sofa/it's hot/he can't speak English/he doesn't have her address.

1. Why's she wearing a ring?
....

2. Why's she opening the window?
....

3. Why can't he understand?
....

4. Why can't he send the postcard to her house?
....

5. Why can't she see it?
....

Unit 26

Language Summary

It's a quarter to one.   *It's twenty-five after one.*

Exercise 1

third *first* ELEVENTH *ninth* sixth tenth twelfth seventh
        FIFTH   EIGHTH   fourth   SECOND

1st *first*	4th	7th	10th ....
2nd *second*	5th	8th	11th ....
3rd	6th	9th	12th ....

Look at this:

It's five after twelve.   It's ten after twelve.   It's a quarter after twelve.   It's twenty after twelve.   It's twenty-five after twelve.   It's twelve-thirty.

It's twenty-five to one.   It's twenty to one.   It's a quarter to one.   It's ten to one.   It's five to one.   It's one o'clock.

SATURDAY'S LATE NIGHT TV

	11:00	11:05	11:15	11:30	11:45	12:00	12:10	12:30	1:00	1:30	2:00
2	NEWS			Sports People			MOVIE: Sullivan's Travels Joel Cray, Veronica Pond				
4	NEWS			Saturday Night Comedy: Millie Tomkins, Host					Talk America		
5	MOVIE: Bathing Beauties Estelle Williams, Jeff Thomas, more.								MOVIE: Don't Look Now Rosie Holt, Bill McGee		
7	NEWS			Hollywood Tonight			MOVIE: Working Melissa Girth, Harry Ford, Sydelle Mills				
9	NEWS	What's Up		Racing Highlights	Wrestling		Best of Midnight				Tomorrow's Headlines

Exercise 2

What time is **the news** *on? It's on at eleven o'clock.*

1. .... *Saturday Night Comedy* ....? ....

2. .... *wrestling* ....? ....

3. .... *Don't Look Now* ....? ....

4. .... *Hollywood Tonight* ....? ....

5. .... *Sports People* ....? ....

6. .... *Talk America* ....? ....

7. .... *What's Up?* ....? ....

8. .... *Bathing Beauties* ....? ....

9. .... *racing* ....? ....

Unit 27

Language Summary

I	'm am	going to	see him	tomorrow.		Am	I	going to	go there?	Yes, I am.
	'm not am not		meet them eat it	next week. next year.		Is	he she it		be there? eat it?	No, I'm not. Yes, she is. No, she isn't.
He She It	's is isn't is not		drink it be here			Are	we you they			Yes, we are. No, they aren't.
We You They	're are aren't are not									

Exercise 1

A: *What's he going to do?*
B: *He's going to open the door.*

1. A: ....
B: ....
....

2. A: ....
B: ....
....

3. A: ....
B: ....
....

Exercise 2

e/Western
What's he going to do? He's going to *watch* a Western.

1. she/magazine
....
....

we/the dishes
....
....

they/football
....
....

4. you/homework
....
....

5. I/a question
....
....

6. Pat/car
....
....

Exercise 3

ennis   *I'm not going to play tennis tomorrow.*
omework   *I'm going to do my homework tomorrow.*
What about you? Write <u>true</u> sentences about tomorrow.

TV.....................................
caviar.....................................
newspaper.....................................

4. rob a bank ....
5. a letter ....

Unit 28

Language Summary

What is she going to	do?
	wear?

SEA GATE MOTEL

Exercise 1

Mr. and Mrs. Ford and their children, Matthew and Amanda, are on vacation. They're standing on the steps outside their motel. In a few minutes they're going to get into their car and drive to the beach.

A. Look at Mrs. Ford.

1. *What's she wearing?*
She's wearing a long dress.
2. *What's she holding?*
She's holding some postcards and a pen.
3. *What's she going to do?*
She's going to write some postcards.

B. Look at Matthew.

1. .... ?

....

....

2. .... ?

....

....

3. .... ?

....

....

C. Look at Amanda.

1. .... ?

....

....

2. .... ?

....

....

3. .... ?

....

D. Look at Mr. Ford.

1. .... ?

....

....

2. .... ?

....

....

3. .... ?

....

Exercise 2

Look at this:

AT THE TOP
ON THE LEFT
IN THE MIDDLE
ON THE RIGHT
AT THE BOTTOM

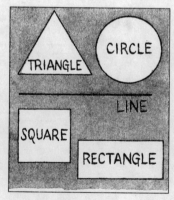

TRIANGLE CIRCLE
LINE
SQUARE RECTANGLE

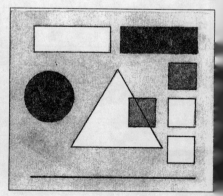

Look at the third picture. It's an abstract painting.
Where's the triangle? It's in the middle.

1. .... circle? ....

2. .... line? ....

3. .... squares? ....

4. .... rectangles? ....

Unit 29

Language Summary

I	like	music.		Do	I	like	music?		Yes, I do./No, I don't.
You	don't like	meat.			you		meat?		Yes, he does./No, he doesn't.
We	do not like	dogs.			we		dogs?		
They					they				
He	likes			Does	he				
She	doesn't like				she				
It	does not like				it				

Last name: *Murphy*
First name(s): *Michael Brian*
Age: *23*
Occupation: *Police officer*
Date:
Signature:

LIKES:
Colors: *red, orange, and green*
Food: *steak, french fries, ice cream*
Drinks: *milk, fruit juice*
Hobbies: *judo, karate, boxing*
DISLIKES:
bad drivers, cheese, dogs, politics

Exercise 1

Look at Michael Murphy.

Does he like dogs?

Write four questions.

1. ....
2. ....
3. ....
4. ....

Exercise 2

He likes steak.

Write four sentences.

1. ....
2. ....
3. ....
4. ....

Exercise 3

He doesn't like bad drivers.

Write three sentences.

1. ....
2. ....
3. ....

Exercise 4

Complete the form below.

Put your picture here.	Last name:	**LIKES:**

Last name: _____
First name(s): _____
Age: _____
Occupation: _____
Date: _____
Signature:

LIKES:
Colors: _____
Food: _____
Drinks: _____
Hobbies: _____
DISLIKES:

Exercise 5

I like carrots.

Write four sentences.

1. ....
2. ....
3. ....
4. ....

Exercise 6

I don't like milk.

Write four sentences.

1. ....
2. ....
3. ....
4. ....

Exercise 7

Do you like ice cream?
Yes, I do or *No, I don't.*
Write true answers.

1. Do you like potatoes? ....
2. Do you like jazz? ....
3. Do you like tea? ....
4. Do you like politics? ....

Unit 30

Language Summary

I need money.
I don't need a big car.
I want a new coat.
I don't want a cup of coffee.
I love my parents.
I don't love him.

Daniel loves Amy.
Who does Daniel love?
He loves Amy.
Who loves Amy?
Daniel does.

Exercise 1

Daniel and Amy are going to get married next week.
They're going to buy a new house. They don't have any
furniture now. They have $6,000 to buy furniture.

Do they need a stove? Yes, they do.
Do they need a stereo? No, they don't.

Write six questions and answers.

1. ....
2. ....
3. ....
4. ....
5. ....
6. ....

Exercise 2

Amy: *We need a bed.*
Daniel: *Right. That's seven hundred and fifty dollars.*
Write four conversations.

1. Amy: ....
   Daniel: ....
2. Amy: ....
   Daniel: ....
3. Amy: ....
   Daniel: ....
4. Amy: ....
   Daniel: ....

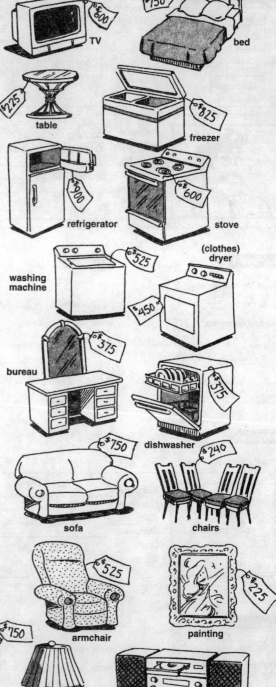

TV $600
bed $750
table $225
freezer $825
refrigerator $900
stove $600
washing machine $525
(clothes) dryer $450
bureau $375
dishwasher $375
sofa $750
chairs $240
armchair $525
painting $225

bookshelf $225
dresser $750
lamp $50
VCR $400
stereo $1,050

Exercise 3

Daniel: *I want a TV set.*
Amy: *Yes, but we don't need a TV set right away.*

1. Daniel: ....

   Amy: ....

2. Daniel: ....

   Amy: ....

3. Daniel: ....

   Amy: ....

4. Daniel: ....

   Amy: ....

Exercise 4

They have $6,000. They can spend only $6,000!

Write sentences.

They need a stove. They can buy one for $600.

1. ....
2. ....
3. ....
4. ....
5. ....

6. ....
7. ....
8. ....
9. ....
10. ....

Total $ .... How much money do they have now? $ ....

Exercise 5

Daniel's going to marry Amy. *He loves her.*

Write sentences.

Melinda's going to marry Josh. ....

Sam's going to marry Tracy. ....

Joe's going to marry Rachel. ....

Kelly's going to marry Wayne. ....

Exercise 6

Who loves Josh? Melinda does.
Who does Melinda love? She loves Josh.

1. .... Tracy.........? ....

2. .... Sam? ....

3. .... Rachel ...... ? ....

4. .... Joe? ....

5. .... Wayne? ....

6. .... Kelly ...... ? ....

Exercise 7

Now you're going to buy a new house. You don't have any furniture either.

You have $6,000.

Look at the picture. What are you going to buy?

I'm going to buy a bed.

1. ....
2. ....

3. ....
4. ....

How much money do you have now? $ ....

Unit 31

Is there a parking lot near here?

Yes. Turn	*right*	*at*	*the first traffic light.*	*Then make a*	*left.*	*It's on the*	*left.*
	left		*the second stop sign.*		*right.*		*right.*

Exercise 1

Look at Unit 31 in the Student Book and complete this conversation.

A: Excuse me.

B: ....

A: I need some dimes.

A: Do you have any change?

B: ....

B: ....

A: Well, could you change a quarter?

Exercise 2

A: ....

B: Good morning.

A: ....

A: .... cassette player?

B: How about next Saturday?

B: Yes, I think so. When do you need it?

A: ....

Exercise 3

A: *Is there a hotel near here?*
B: *Yes, there is. Take the second right, then walk straight ahead, and it's on your left.*

Now write conversations with: parking lot/supermarket/post office/bank/
bus stop/public telephone/coffee shop/shopping mall.

1. A: ....

   B: ....

5. A: ....

   B: ....

2. A: ....

   B: ....

6. A: ....

   B: ....

3. A: ....

   B: ....

7. A: ....

   B: ....

4. A: ....

   B: ....

8. A: ....

   B: ....

Unit 32

Language Summary

What	do	you they	do every day?
	does	he she	

What time	do	you they	do that?
	does	he	

Exercise 1

What time do you wake up?
I wake up at seven o'clock.

2. What time do you have breakfast?
....

4. What time do you have dinner?
....

1. What time do you get up?
....

3. What time do you have lunch?
....

5. What time do you go to bed?
....

Exercise 2

Do you read *The Los Angeles Times*?　　No, I don't.
Do you get up at 7:30?　　Yes, I do.

1. Do you read a newspaper?..

2. Do you go to bed at eleven o'clock?..

3. Do you rest after lunch?..

4. Do you dress for dinner?..

5. Do you have dinner at eight o'clock? ....

6. Do you have breakfast in bed? ....

Exercise 3

Now write the questions in this conversation.

: ....

: Hmm...I get up at seven o'clock.

: ....

: I have breakfast at 7:30.

: ....

: I leave home at eight o'clock.

A: ....

B: I get to school at 8:30.

A: ....

B: I have lunch at 12:30.

A: ....

B: I go to bed at eleven o'clock.

Exercise 4

Complete the spaces. Use these words: in/until/at/before/at/to/after/in/on.

"...live .... Houston. I get up .... eight o'clock, and I take a bath .... breakfast. .... breakfast, I leave ...me and catch a bus .... the office. .... Saturday and Sunday I don't get up .... eight o'clock. I stay .... bed .... nine o'clock, and I read the newspaper."

Exercise 5

...ordinary day　　*a pink house*
...ntinue.

1. .... American movie　**2.** .... silver earring　**3.** .... economical car　**4.** .... pink pants suit

5. .... ugly boxer　**6.** .... boring book　**7.** .... interesting job　**8.** .... leather purse

9. .... hotel manager　**10.** .... orange chair　**11.** .... ID card　**12.** .... famous actor

13. .... beautiful woman　**14.** .... old necklace　**15.** .... silk shirt　**16.** .... electric stove

17. .... new umbrella　**18.** .... busy office　**19.** .... airport bus　**20.** .... international hotel

Unit 33

Arnold Rivera interviews a famous person every week for the television program *Real People*.

Exercise 1

NOTES: Darryl Nelson
1. Guitarist for *Manhattan Ravers*.
2. Live/apartment in New York.
3. Get up/11:15.
4. Read *The Post*.
5. Arrive at the studio/3:30.
6. Leave the studio/midnight.
7. Have dinner/12:30.
8. Go to bed/three o'clock.

1. *He's a guitarist for* Manhattan Ravers.
2. *He lives in an apartment in New York.*

Continue.

3. ....
4. ....
5. ....

6. ....
7. ....
8. ....

Exercise 2

NOTES: Sandra Woo
1. Reporter for WCOV-TV in Chicago.
2. Live/house Evanston.
3. Get up/nine o'clock
4. Read *The Chicago Sun Times*.
5. Arrive at TV station/1:30.
6. Have dinner/six o'clock.
7. Leave TV station/11:15.
8. Go to bed/midnight.

Write questions and answers.

1. *What does she do? She's a TV reporter.*
2. *Where does she live? She lives in a house in Evanston.*

3. ....
4. ....
5. ....
6. ....
7. ....
8. ....

Exercise 3

NOTES: Darryl Goodman
1. Baseball player for Los Angeles Dodgers.
2. Live/new house in Beverly Hills.
3. Get up/6:30.
4. Read *The Los Angeles Times*.
5. Arrive at the stadium/eight o'clock.
6. Leave the stadium/2:30.
7. Have dinner/5:30.
8. Go to bed/9:30.

Write questions and answers.

1. ....
2. ....
3. ....
4. ....
5. ....
6. ....
7. ....
8. ....

Exercise

Look at these people:

LAST NAME Talbot

FIRST NAME(S) June

AGE 22

OCCUPATION Flight
             attendant

LAST NAME Martello

FIRST NAME(S) Paul Anthony

AGE 51

OCCUPATION Farmer

LAST NAME Rodriguez

FIRST NAME(S) Maria Teresa

AGE 44

OCCUPATION Doctor

Now look at the sentences below. Read <u>all</u> of them carefully. There are 24 sentences. Put them in the correct columns. Put eight in each column.

1.	1.	1. ....
2.	2.	2. ....
3.	3.	3. ....
4.	4.	4. ....
5.	5.	5. ....
6.	6.	6. ....
7.	7.	7. ....
8.	8.	8. ....

I'm strong.

I work outside.

I speak two languages.

I wear a white coat.

I have a receptionist.

I don't wear a uniform.

I get a big salary.

I meet a lot of famous people.

I get up very early.

I can read some Latin.

I go to Seattle every week.

I work in a hospital.

I work with animals.

I travel in my job.

I wear glasses.

I work on a farm.

I live in the suburbs.

I wear a uniform.

I live in the country.

I have a truck.

I live near the airport.

I'm young.

I stay in a lot of hotels.

I have a lot of diplomas.

Unit 35

Language Summary

I	always	get up	at seven o'clock.
You	usually		
We	often		
They	sometimes		
	occasionally		
He	hardly ever	gets up	
She	never		

Exercise 1

Complete the sentences with: always/usually/often/
sometimes/occasionally/hardly ever/never.

1. He likes football. He watches a lot of football games on TV.

   He .... watches football games.

2. She goes to the movies four or five times a year.

   She .... goes to the movies.

3. I like classical music, and I like jazz.

   I .... listen to jazz, and I

   .... listen to classical music.

4. They don't like meat. They're vegetarians.

   They .... eat meat.

5. Every morning she drinks coffee.

   She .... drinks coffee.

6. He doesn't usually drink wine, but at Christmas he has a
   glass of wine with dinner.

   He .... drinks wine.

7. They go to bed at eleven o'clock from Sunday to Friday,
   but on Saturday they go to bed at midnight.

   They .... go to bed at eleven o'clock.

Exercise 2

Do you listen to classical music? *Sometimes.*
Do you eat meat? *Never.*

1. Do you drink coffee? ....

2. Do you play golf? ....

3. Do you go to the movies? ....

4. Do you eat chocolate? ....

5. Do you get up early? ....

6. Do you eat potatoes?...

7. Do you watch TV? ....

8. Do you drink cola?...

9. Do you go to bed early?..

10. Do you go to rock concerts?...

Exercise 3

What about <u>you</u>? Write true sentences using: always/
usually/often/sometimes/occasionally/hardly ever/never.

1. ....

2. ....

3. ....

4. ....

5. ....

6. ....

7. ....

Exercise 4

Now write seven sentences about <u>your teacher</u> using the
same words.

1. ....

2. ....

3. ....

4. ....

5. ....

6. ....

7. ....

Unit 36

Language Summary

What time	do you	usually have dinner?	How often	do you	go out?	
When	does she			does she		
			Do you	ever	go to the theater?	
What	do you	usually do after dinner?	Does she	often		
	does she					

Exercise 1

you/the movies   *How often do you go to the movies?*
she/steak   *How often does she eat steak?*
Now write the questions.

1. he /a newspaper

....?

2. she /milk shake

.... ?

3. they/tennis

.... ?

4. you/TV

.... ?

5. she /radio

.... ?

6. he /the theater

.... ?

Exercise 2

Look at this:

once	a day	often
twice	a week	
three times	a month	
ten times	a year	never

Now answer these questions.

1. How often do you brush your teeth?

....

2. How often do you polish your shoes?

....

3. How often do you wash your hair?

....

4. How often do you write a letter?

....

5. How often do you go to the bank?

....

6. How often do you go to the dentist?

....

Exercise 3

Look at this:

Yes,		No,	
	often.		not often.
	sometimes.		hardly ever.
	occasionally.		never.

Now write questions and answers.

wash the dishes	wear boots	go swimming	vacuum the carpet

A: *Do you ever wash the dishes?*
B: *Yes, sometimes.*

1. A: ....
.... ?
B: ....

2. A: ....
.... ?
B: ....

3. A: ....
.... ?
B: ....

Unit 37

Language Summary

I	walk to work.
	walk to work every day.
	usually walk to work.

I'm	walking to work.
	walking to work now.
	walking to work right now.

What	do you	do every day?
	does he	

What	's he	doing	now?
	are you		

Exercise

Look at the first picture. Look at the example. Look at the sentences at the bottom of the page. Read all of the sentences carefully. Write two sentences under each picture.

A. Paul's a student.
B. *He goes to college.*
C. *He's playing football.*

1. A. Deborah's a doctor.
B. ....
C. ....

2. A. Brian and Brad are factory workers.
B. ....
C. ....

3. A. Crystal's a television reporter.
B. ....
C. ....

4. A. Joseph's a pilot.
B. ....
C. ....

5. A. Sonia's an artist.
B. ....
C. ....

6. A. Karen and Patrick are teachers.
B. ....
C. ....

He's dancing.

They make cars.

✓ He's playing football.

She's riding a bicycle.

She interviews famous people.

He flies Boeing 747s.

They teach in a high school.

She's cooking.

✓ He goes to college.

She's playing the piano.

She paints pictures.

They're correcting homework.

They're lying on a beach.

She works in a hospital.

Unit 38

Language Summary

How	do	you	do that?
		we	
		they	
	does	he	
		she	

I	do	this	well.
You			badly.
We			carefully.
They			carelessly.
He	does		slowly.
She			fast.

He's a good singer./He sings well.
They're bad players./They play badly.

She's a careful driver./She drives carefully.
I'm a slow driver./I drive slowly.

Exercise 1

bad	*badly*		happy	*happily*		good	*well*
slow	....		busy	....		fast	
careful	....		noisy	....		hard	....
careless	....		lucky	....			
beautiful	....		angry	....			
quiet	....						
wonderful	....						
intelligent	....						
sad	....						

Exercise 2

They play well.   *They're good players.*

1. She sings badly.   ....

2. He dances well.   ....

3. They swim badly.   ....

4. She teaches well.   ....

5. They ski well.   ....

6. He drives badly.   ....

Exercise 3

How's he playing?
He's playing well.

1. .... ?

....

2. .... ?

....

3. .... ?

....

Exercise 4

He's a good player. *He plays well.*
She's a bad singer. *She sings badly.*

1. He's a careful driver.   ....

2. ....   They drive carefully.

3. I'm a hard worker.   ....

4. She's a fast typist.   ....

5. ....   He dances beautifully.

6. ....   She drives slowly.

Unit 39

Language Summary

When is it?	On	Sunday	night.

What	am	I	doing	tomorrow?
	are	you		next week?
		we		next month?
		they		on Monday?
	is	he		on Saturday?
		she		

I	'm	going	out of town.
	am		to Washington, D.C.
We	're		to Florida.
You	are		
They			
He	's		
She	is		

	Would you like to	go to	a movie?
			a baseball game?
		have	dinner?

Exercise 1

FOOTBALL GAME
★ SATURDAY, 3:00 PM ★

A: Would you like to go to a football game?
B: When is it?
A: On Saturday afternoon.

Dance
Tuesday, 8:00 pm

1. A: ....
....
B: ....
A: ....

ROCK CONCERT
FRIDAY, 8:30 PM

2. A: ....
....
B: ....
A: ....

Picnic
SUNDAY, 2:00 – 5:00 PM

3. A: ....
....
B: ....
A: ....

Party Thursday, 7:30 pm

4. A: ....
....
B: ....
A: ....

BARBECUE
Saturday, 12:30 pm

5. A: ....
....
B: ....
A: ....

Exercise 2

Lisa/tomorrow

1. A: What's she doing tomorrow?
B: She's going out of town.
A: Where's she going?
B: She's going to San Francisco.
A: For how long?
B: Just for three days.

Anthony/on Sunday

2. A: ....
B: ....
A: ....
B: ....
A: ....
B: ....

Tiffany and Brandon/next Friday

3. A: ....
B: ....
A: ....
B: ....
A: ....
B: ....

Exercise 3

Look at the third conversation in the Student Book. Complete this conversation.

A: .... dance?
B: Sure.
A: .... often?
B: Sometimes.

A: .... near here?
B: No, I live in Dallas.
A: .... work?
B: In a hospital.

Unit 40

Language Summary

Excuse	me,	how do I get to	the Canadian Falls?
Pardon		where can I find	
		I'm looking for	the Skylon Tower.

| Where are | the American Falls? |

| It's | behind | you. |
| | in front of | |

| They're | across | the bridge. |
| | on | your right. |

Exercise 1

Look at the map and give directions to the three people.
Look at the conversations in the Student Book to help you.

A: Excuse me, how do I get to the Riverside Restaurant.

B: ....

....

....

A: Excuse me. Where can I find the river boat trips?

B: ....

....

....

A: Pardon me. I'm looking for the Fairfield Hotel.

B: ....

....

....

Look at this:

13th	thirteen	20th	twentieth	26th	twenty-sixth
14th	fourteenth	21st	twenty-first	27th	twenty-seventh
15th	fifteenth	22nd	twenty-second	28th	twenty-eighth
16th	sixteenth	23rd	twenty-third	29th	twenty-ninth
17th	seventeenth	24th	twenty-fourth	30th	thirtieth
18th	eighteenth	25th	twenty-fifth	31st	thirty-first
19th	nineteenth				

Exercise 2

12/21   *December 21st*

1. 3/18 ....

2. 7/26 ....

3. 11/19 ....

4. 1/13 ....

5. 4/20 ....

6. 12/11 ....

7. 6/23 ....

8. 5/22 ....

9. 10/31 ....

10. 2/15 ....

11. 3/23 ....

12. 4/8 ....

New American STREAMLINE

BERNARD HARTLEY & PETER VINEY

DEPARTURES

An intensive American English series for beginners
Workbook B
Units 41–80
REVISED BY TIM FALLA

Oxford University Press

Oxford University Press

198 Madison Avenue
New York, NY 10016 USA

Great Clarendon Street
Oxford OX2 6DP England

Oxford   New York
Athens   Auckland   Bangkok   Bogota   Bombay
Buenos Aires   Calcutta   Cape Town   Dar es Salaam
Delhi   Florence   Hong Kong   Istanbul   Karachi
Kuala Lumpur   Madras   Madrid   Melbourne
Mexico City   Nairobi   Paris   Singapore
Taipei   Tokyo   Toronto   Warsaw

and associated companies in
Berlin   Ibadan

OXFORD is a trademark of Oxford University Press.

ISBN 0-19-434837-7 (Workbook B)

Copyright © 1995 B. Hartley, P. Viney, and Oxford
University Press

Based on the original American adaptation by
Flamm/Northam Authors and Publishers Services, Inc.

Editorial Manager: Susan Lanzano
Editor: Ken Mencz
Designer: Harry Katz/John Daly
Senior Art Buyer: Alexandra F. Rockafellar
Production Manager: Abram Hall

Cover illustration by: Pete Kelly

Illustrations and realia by: Carlos Castellanos, John Daly,
Dee DeLoy, Jenny Dubnau, Rich Garramone,
Sandy Hoffman, Claudia Kehrhahn, Paddy Mounter,
Debra Page-Trim, Tom Powers, David Slonim, Anne
Stanley, William Waitzman, Rose Zgodzinski

Printing (last digit) 10 9 8 7 6 5

Printed in Hong Kong.

TO THE TEACHER

Workbook B of *New American Streamline: Departures* consists of forty units. Each unit relates directly to the corresponding unit in the Student Book of *New American Streamline: Departures*, units 41–80.

The Workbook is an optional component of the series, designed to provide language summaries and additional written exercises. It may be used in the following ways:

1. In more extensive courses as additional classroom material, providing extra oral practice and written reinforcement and consolidation of the basic core material in the Student Book.
2. As homework material in more intensive situations.

The Workbook should only be used after full oral practice of the corresponding unit in the Student Book. The language summaries provide material for review.

Another workbook is available for units 1–40 of the Student Book, under the title *Workbook A*.

Bernard Hartley
Peter Viney

Unit 41

Exercise 1

Write the questions.

Last name	
First name(s)	
Address	*Where do you live?*
Date of birth	
Occupation	

Exercise 2

Put the sentences in the correct order to make a conversation. Write 1–6 in the boxes.

☐ Great. Can you complete this form?
  I also need a passport photo and $20.
☐ Hello. I'd like a membership card for the
  Recreation Center.
☐ It's right here.
☐ I live here.
☐ Do you live, work, or go to school
  in the area?
☐ OK. Do you have a driver's license?

Exercise 3

Complete this form.

WEST SIDE RECREATION CENTER

Last Name _____   First Name _____

Title _____   Date of Birth _____

Address _____

Occupation _____

Signature _____   Date _____

Exercise 4

Look at the second conversation in the Student Book. Complete this conversation.

A: … so, are you a student here?

B: Yes. ....

A: ....?

B: E.S.L.

A: Really? ....?

B: Seoul in Korea.

A: Are ....?

B: No, I'm not. ....

Unit 42

Language Summary

I	was	here.	Was	I	here?	Yes,	I	was.	No,	I	wasn't.
He	wasn't	there.		he	there?		he			he	
She	was not			she			she			she	
It				it			it			it	
You	were		Were	you			we	were.		we	weren't.
We	weren't			we			you			you	
They	were not			they			they			they	

MMI
Mechanical Music Inc.
Artist   *Michael Jackman*
World Tour
(Last Year)

January:	*the United States and Mexico*
February:	*Central America*
April:	*South America*
June:	*Australia*
August:	*Japan*
September:	*Europe*
December:	*Canada*

MMI
Mechanical Music Inc.
Artist   *Technocrat*
West Coast Concert Tour
(Last Week)

Monday:	*Seattle*
Tuesday:	*Portland*
Wednesday:	*Sacramento*
Thursday:	*San Francisco*
Friday:	*Monterey*
Saturday:	*Los Angeles*
Sunday:	*San Diego*

MMI
Mechanical Music Inc.
Artist   *Tracy Champion*
Schedule for visit
to New York (Yesterday)

7 AM:	*on the "Today Show"*
9 AM:	*at RCA Records*
1 PM:	*at Sardi's restaurant*
3 PM:	*in her hotel room*
5 PM:	*at a press party*
8 PM:	*at Carnegie Hall*
12 AM:	*in bed*

Exercise

Where was he in January?
He was in the United States and Mexico.
Continue.

1. ....
2. ....
3. ....
4. ....
5. ....
6. ....

Where were they on Monday?
They were in Seattle.

1. ....
2. ....
3. ....
4. ....
5. ....
6. ....

Where was she at seven o'clock?
She was on the "Today Show."

1. ....
2. ....
3. ....
4. ....
5. ....
6. ....

Look at this:

today ... yesterday

this morning ... yesterday morning

this afternoon ... yesterday afternoon

this evening ... yesterday evening

this week ... last week

this month ... last month

this year ... last year

tonight ... last night

Language Summary

There	was wasn't	a restaurant.
	were	some hotels.
	weren't	any buses.

| Was there a beach? | Yes, there was. No, there wasn't. |
| Were there any stores? | Yes, there were. No, there weren't. |

| What | was | it | like? |
| | were | they the people | |

| It | was | great. |
| They | were | boring. |

ADVERTISEMENT
COME TO

SAFARI PARK

You can drive into new Safari Park and see the animals from your car.
It isn't a zoo. The animals run free. Don't open your car door!

- Elephants
- Lions
- Tigers
- Giraffes
- Zebras
- Kangaroos
- A Restaurant
- An Aquarium
- A Swimming Pool
- A Picnic Area
- A Souvenir Shop

Exercise 1

Jennifer was there last Sunday. Her friend is asking her about it.

Were there any elephants?
Was there a restaurant?

Write eight more questions.

1. .... 5. ....
2. .... 6. ....
3. .... 7. ....
4. .... 8. ....

Exercise 2

There was a restaurant.
There were some elephants.

Write eight sentences.

1. .... 5. ....
2. .... 6. ....
3. .... 7. ....
4. .... 8. ....

Exercise 3

There wasn't a museum.
There weren't any alligators.

Now write sentences with: a tennis court/a beach/cats/gorillas/a hotel/dogs.

1. .... 4. ....
2. .... 5. ....
3. .... 6. ....

Unit 44

Language Summary

I	had	breakfast.		Did	I	have	breakfast?		Yes, I did.
You	did not have	a cola.			you		a cola?		No, I didn't.
He	didn't have	dinner.			he		any food?		
She					she				
We					we				
They					they				

Exercise 1

2. a haircut   **4.** a party   **6.** a cup of coffee

an aspirin   ....
I didn't have an aspirin yesterday.   ....
a headache
I had a headache yesterday.

Now write true sentences.

1. a cola   **3.** an English lesson   **5.** a doctor's appointment   **7.** a hamburger

....

....

Exercise 2

He always has coffee at eleven o'clock.
So yesterday *he had coffee at eleven o'clock.*
They never have a class on Sundays.
So last Sunday *they didn't have a class.*

Now write sentences.

1. She never has vacation in June. So last June....................

....

2. We always have lunch at 12:30. So yesterday ....

....

3. They always have a cup of coffee in the morning. So

yesterday morning...

....

4. He never has a good time on Saturdays. So last Saturday

....

5. She never has breakfast on weekends. So last weekend

....

Exercise 3

Answer these questions, with *Yes, I did* or *No, I didn't.*

1. Did you have breakfast at eight o'clock yesterday? ....

2. Did you have a cup of coffee this morning? ....

3. Did you have a birthday party last year? ....

4. Did you have any homework last night?...

Exercise 4

Answer these questions.

1. What time did you have breakfast yesterday?...

2. Who did you have breakfast with?...

3. Did you have some orange juice this morning? ....

4. Did you have any tea yesterday? ....

5. Did you have a cold last week? ....

6. How much homework did you have last night? ....

Unit 45

Language Summary

I	went	to school.	Did	I	come	to school	yesterday?		Present	Past
You	didn't go	home.		you	go	home	last week?		am/is	was
He	did not go			he			at 7 o'clock?		are	were
She	came			she			on Tuesday?		have/has	had
We	didn't come			we					go	went
They	did not come			they					come	came
									get	got

I	got	a letter	yesterday.	Did	I	get	a letter?
You	didn't get		last Thursday.		you		
He	did not get		this morning.		he		
She					she		
We					we		
They					they		

Look at the shopping list.
Mrs. Scott went to town yesterday afternoon.

Butcher	Drugstore
steak	shampoo
hamburgers	razor blades
Bakery	Supermarket
bread	milk
rolls	apples

Exercise 1

A: *She went to the butcher.*
B: *She got some steak and some hamburgers.*

Write six more sentences.

1. A: ....
   B: ....
   ....

2. A: ....   3. A: ....
   B: ....   B: ....
   ....

Exercise 2

lamb   *She didn't get any lamb.*

Write sentences with: doughnuts/soap/oranges.

1. .... 2. .... 3. ....

Exercise 3

A: *How much steak did she get?*
B: *How many hamburgers did she get?*   2. A: ....

Write questions.   B: ....

1. A: ....   3. A: ....
   B: ....   B: ....

Look at this:

by taxi
by bus
by train
by bicycle
on foot

Exercise 4

he/taxi   *He came by taxi.*

Write sentences.

1. they/bus ....
2. she/foot ....
3. we/train ....
4. I/bicycle ....

Unit 46

Language Summary

I	finished	the letter.	Did	I	finish	the letter?	Yes, I did.	Where	did	they	go?
You	didn't finish	it.		you	type	it?	No, I didn't.	What		she	see?
He	typed			he	photocopy						
She	didn't type			she				What time		he	arrive?
We	photocopied			we				When		I	leave?
They	didn't photocopy			they							

Exercise 1

Look at this:

Look at these words.
visit/smile/look/study/watch/listen/dictate/start/play/like/rest/
love/carry/wash/want/need/dress/repeat/rent/stop

Now write them in the correct place, in the same way as
the examples.

finish ... finished
sign ... signed
mail ... mailed

....

....

....

....

....

....

....

type ... typed
telephone ... telephoned
reserve ... reserved

stay ... stayed
enjoy ... enjoyed

....

....

....

....

....

....

....

....

photocopy ... photocopied

....

drop ... dropped

....

Exercise 2

He dictated a letter. What *did he dictate?*

Continue.

1. She played tennis in the park.

   Where ....?

2. He carried three suitcases.

   How many ....?

3. They started at six o'clock.

   What time ....?

4. She rented the car on Saturday.

   When ....?

5. He repeated the exercise.

   Why ....?

6. They stayed in a hotel.

   Which ....?

Exercise 3

Tony/Ryan/finish/test
Tony finished the test, but Ryan didn't finish it.

Continue.

Keiko/Ana/like/movie ....

Andrea/John/study/vocabulary ....

Chelsea/Ben/watch/program ....

THE STORY OF CONNIE & CLIVE

CONNIE AND CLIVE .... IN SUNSHINE CITY EARLY ONE MORNING.

THEY .... THEIR CAR OUTSIDE THE BANK.

CLIVE .... INTO THE BANK. CONNIE .... IN THE CAR AND .... THE STREET.

CLIVE .... FOR A FEW MINUTES AND .... CAREFULLY AROUND THE BANK.

SUDDENLY HE .... OUT A GUN.

CLIVE .... A WOMAN .... NOBODY ....

THE MANAGER .... OUT OF HIS OFFICE.

THE MANAGER ....

CLIVE .... COLDLY.

THE MANAGER .... THE SAFE, AND .... AN ALARM BELL UNDER THE COUNTER.

THE BELL WAS VERY LOUD. CLIVE .... AFRAID. HE .... THREE TIMES AND .... THE MANAGER.

AT THAT MOMENT TWO POLICEMEN .... INTO THE BANK. CLIVE .... HIS GUN. THEY .... HIM.

CONNIE WAS OUTSIDE. SHE .... THE CAR, AND SHE ....!

Now put these words in the correct places:
waited/arrested/pulled/arrived/moved/looked/rushed/was/parked/started/stayed/killed/replied/hurried/walked/pushed/asked/opened/fired/shouted/escaped/dropped/watched/screamed.

Unit 48

Language Summary

Present	Past		Present	Past		Present	Past
see	saw		fly	flew		ride	rode
eat	ate		shine	shone		buy	bought
drink	drank		meet	met		bring	brought
take	took		write	wrote			

Exercise 1

Look at this information about three vacations last year.

	Heather	Rick	Jerome and Noreen
Place	Mexico City	Los Angeles	Paris
Travel	AeroMexico	TWA	Air France
Food	Enchiladas	Steak	Chicken with lemon sauce
Drink	Coffee	Coca-Cola	Mineral water
Important place	The Aztec pyramids	Disneyland	The Eiffel Tower
Souvenir	A big Mexican hat	A movie poster	Some perfume

Heather went to Mexico City last year. She flew with AeroMexico.
She ate enchiladas and drank coffee. She saw the Aztec pyramids.
She bought a big Mexican hat.

1. Write about Rick.

....

....

....

....

2. Write about Jerome and Noreen.

....

....

....

....

Exercise 2

Complete the sentences. Use the past tense of the words in the box.

come	write
ride	shine
send	bring
go	meet
take	is
see	

Steven .... to India last summer. He .... a lot of people there. He .... a lot of letters and .... them to all his friends. The sun .... nearly every day. It .... very hot. He .... the Taj Mahal, and he .... on an elephant. He .... a lot of photos. He .... home with Air-India. He .... a lot of souvenirs with him.

Exercise 3

Answer these questions.

1. Where did you go on your last vacation? ....

....

2. How did you go there? ....

....

3. What did you see there? ....

....

4. What did you eat? ....

....

5. What did you drink? ....

....

6. What did you buy? ....

....

7. How did you come home? ....

....

8. Did you send any postcards? ....

....

9. Did you take any photographs? ....

....

10. Did it rain? ....

....

Unit 49

Language Summary

I You We They	have had	only	a little	food. water. gas.
			a few	crackers. books.
He She It	has had			

I You We They	don't have didn't have	much	food. water.
		many	crackers. books.
He She It	doesn't have didn't have		

Roy Weston is a scientist. He's crossing Antarctica. Yesterday he visited a famous place. Major William Campbell, the famous explorer, stayed there in 1921 with five of his men. They were there for six weeks. They didn't move because of the weather. The Antarctic winter killed them. Roy has a book about Campbell. In the book, there is a picture of a note. Campbell wrote it. He died the next day.

> 7/10/21. We arrived here exactly six weeks ago. We have only a little food left.
> We have   1 box of crackers
>   ½ a bar of chocolate
>   a small piece of meat
>   1 can of beans
>   ½ a jar of coffee
> We also have 1 box of matches (wet)
>   ½ liter of kerosene
>   two pieces of wood
> The weather is cold. It is still snowing
> It is too cold for us — I can't write —

Exercise 1

They had some crackers, but they didn't have many.
They had some chocolate, but they didn't have much.
Write six sentences.

1. ....
2. ....
3. ....

4. ....
5. ....
6. ....

Exercise 2

They had only a few crackers.
They had only a little chocolate.
Write six sentences.

1. ....
2. ....
3. ....
4. ....
5. ....
6. ....

Exercise 3

How many crackers did they have?
How much chocolate did they have?
Write six questions.

1. ....
2. ....
3. ....
4. ....
5. ....
6. ....

Exercise 4

Write answers.

1. Who's Roy Weston? ....

2. What's he doing? ....

3. How many men were with Major Campbell? ....

4. How many weeks were they there? ....

5. What killed them? ....

6. Who wrote the note? ....

7. What's the date on the note? ....

8. What date did Campbell die? ....

Unit 50

Language Summary

I	sang	well.
You	danced	badly.
He	played	carefully.
She		quickly.
We		
They		

Exercise 1

Look at this:

go *went*   catch *caught*   Now write the past of these verbs:

eat	come	dictate	write	has	drink
....	....	....	....	....	....
sing	bring	buy	shine	are	hurry
....	....	....	....	....	....
carry	see	meet	take	send	drop
....	....	....	....	....	....
enjoy					
....					

Exercise 2

He's a bad singer.
He usually sings badly, but yesterday he sang well!

1. They're slow workers.

....

....

2. He's a careless writer.

....

....

3. They're good players.

....

....

Exercise 3

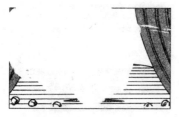

April's a beautiful dancer.
She always dances beautifully.

1. Keith's a careful driver.

....

2. Frank and Sonia are good singers.

....

3. Robert's a slow typist.

....

4. Pat's a bad player.

....

Unit 51

Language Summary

I	did	that	an hour	ago.
You	saw	them	two days	
We	bought		five minutes	
They			three weeks	
He				
She				

Present	Past
find	found
give	gave
leave	left
lose	lost

Exercise 1

Mr. and Mrs. Mason are from London. Last week they were on vacation in Florida. Today is Sunday, August 12.

Yesterday they flew home.

Make more sentences.

1. *Two days ago* ....

2. *Three days ago* ....

3. ....

4. ....

5. ....

6. ....

Week-at-a-glance

Sun 5	*Arrive in Orlando*
Mon 6	*Meet Aunt Emily*
Tue 7	*Go to beach*
Wed 8	*Visit Disney-MGM Studios*
Thu 9	*Buy souvenirs*
Fri 10	*Drive to Tampa*
Sat 11	*Fly home*

Exercise 2

Look at this:

A: *I went to Philadelphia last week.*
B: *Really? How did you go?*
A: *I went by train.*
B: *How long did it take?*
A: *It took an hour and eight minutes.*

Now write conversations for: Baltimore and Washington.

1. A: ....
   B: ....
   A: ....
   B: ....
   A: ....

2. A: ....
   B: ....
   A: ....
   B: ....
   A: ....

U.S. RAIL ★★★★

U.S. RAIL CITYLINER SERVICE

Morning Express Trains
New York to Washington, DC, and two intermediate cities.

TRAIN NO.	291	281
New York, NY	8:00 AM	9:00 AM
Philadelphia, PA	9:08 AM	10:08 AM
Baltimore, MD	10:17 AM	11:17 AM
Washington, DC	10:49 AM	11:49 AM

Exercise 3

Mileage & driving time from Los Angeles to selected cities

	Miles	Driving time
San Francisco	436	7h 16m
San Diego	127	2h 15m
Las Vegas	276	5h 55m
Phoenix	436	7h 35m
h = hours	m = minutes	

How many miles is it from Los Angeles to San Francisco?
It's 436 miles.

Continue.

1. ....San Diego?
....

2. ....Las Vegas?
....

3. ....Phoenix?
....

Exercise 4

A: *How long does it take to drive to San Francisco from Los Angeles?*
B: *Seven hours and sixteen minutes.*

Now write sentences for: San Diego, Las Vegas, Phoenix.

1. A: ....

....

 B: ....

2. A: ....

....

 B: ....

3. A: ....

....

 B: ....

Exercise 5

It's five o'clock now.
The Lost and Found Department is closing.
The clerk is looking at the lost and found book.

A. *Alice Gosak left an umbrella on bus M14.*
B. *Bud Smith found it.*
C. *I gave it to Ms. Gosak two hours ago.*

Now write sentences about the other things.

1. A. ....
 B. ....
 C. ....
2. A. ....
 B. ....
 C. ....
3. A. ....
 B. ....
 C. ....

CITY BUS COMPANY

LOST & FOUND DEPARTMENT

DATE: Tuesday, 4/10

	ITEM	TURNED IN		PICKED UP	
No.	Description	Driver	Bus	Owner	Time
1.	umbrella	Bud Smith	M14	*Alice Gosak*	3:00
2.	briefcase	Lucy Green	E72	*Mrs. J.J. Lawrence*	4:00
3.	gold pen	Beau Garland	B4	*William P. Wilson*	4:30
4.	purse	Joe Garcia	DD1	*Laura Holzberg*	4:45

Exercise 6

Now complete this conversation.

A: Where did you go last weekend?

B: .... Las Vegas.

A: Oh, ...?

B: I went by car.

A: ....?

B: About six hours.

Unit 52

Language Summary

Present	Past		Present	Past		Present	Past		Present	Past
begin	began		fall	fell		meet	met		snow	snowed
burn	burned		find	found		open	opened		speak	spoke
destroy	destroyed		leave	left		send	sent		spend	spent

Exercise 1

Look at this:

leave   *left*

Continue.

is	get	stay	lose	play
....	....	....	....	....

give	travel	forget	spend	find
....	....	....	....	....

ride	are	fall	leave	fly
....	....	....	....	....

WCOV-TV NEWS

Date: Thursday, October 21
Anchor: Paula Fredericks
Notes: 1

Explosion/Tapatipa/capital/Volonia
destroy/hundreds of houses
apartment buildings/burn down
army/city
help/survivors
Red Cross/send/planes/tents/food/
area/this morning

WCOV-TV NEWS

Notes: 2

Indian Army/five climbers/Himalayas
leave/last month/Mount Everest
snow heavily/three days ago
army/some soldiers/two days ago
they/two nights/mountains/
not find climbers

WCOV-TV NEWS

Notes: 3

Boston Mayor/Betty Trimm/
high school/Dorchester/yesterday
meet/teachers/speak/students
do/work/education

Exercise 2

Look at the notes. Look at the example. Look at Unit 52 in the Student Book.
Write the news for October 21.

1. *Last night there was an explosion in Tapatipa, the capital of Volonia. The explosion destroyed hundreds of houses. Many apartment buildings burned down. The Volonian army is in the city. They are helping survivors. The Red Cross sent planes with tents and food to the area this morning.*

2. ....
....
....
....
....
....
....
....

3. ....
....
....
....
....
....
....
....

Unit 53

Language Summary

Who	graduated	in 1991?	Present	Past	Present	Past	Present	Past	Present	Past
Who	graduated	in 1991?	adopt	adopted	drive	drove	investigate	investigated	marry	married
Where	was	she born?	become	became	emigrate	emigrated	like	liked	remove	removed
When	did	she start school?	call	called	graduate	graduated	live	lived	telephone	telephoned
Did	she go	into the hospital?	die	died	hear	heard	major	majored		

Exercise 1

Look at this:

drive   *drove*

Continue.

spend	rescue	photocopy	work	crash
....	....	....	....	....

speak	send	open	dance	happen
....	....	....	....	....

destroy	begin	fall	tour	visit
....	....	....	....	....

Exercise 2

A. He went to Houston.
B. *Did he go to Houston?*
C. *He didn't go to* Dallas.
D. When *did he go to Houston?*

A. It was a sunny day.
B. *Was it a sunny day?*
C. *It wasn't a* rainy day.
D. What *was it like?*

1. A. They flew to New York.
B. ....?
C. .... Chicago.
D. How ....?

2. A. She graduated from Yale.
B. ....?
C. .... Harvard.
D. When ....?

3. A. He drove very quickly.
B. ....?
C. .... slowly.
D. How ....?

4. A. It was a green hat.
B. ....?
C. .... brown hat.
D. What color ....?

5. A. John Lennon died in 1980.
B. ....?
C. .... 1975.
D. When ....?

6. A. They emigrated to England.
B. ....?
C. .... Australia.
D. Who ....?

7. A. She wrote home every week.
B. ....?
C. .... every day.
D. How often ....?

8. A. He sent her a fax.
B. ....?
C. .... a letter.
D. Why ....?

9. A. He got up at 10:00.
B. ....?
C. .... noon.
D. What time ....?

10. A. The trip took five hours.
B. ....?
C. .... five minutes.
D. How long ....?

11. A. She gave me some money.
B. ....?
C. .... food.
D. Who ....?

12. A. She majored in French.
B. ....?
C. .... German.
D. What ....?

13. A. He forgot his Workbook.
B. ....?
C. .... Student Book.
D. Why ....?

14. A. She bought some books.
B. ....?
C. .... records.
D. What ....?

15. A. Jack London was born in 1876.
B. ....?
C. .... 1976.
D. When ....?

Unit 54

Language Summary

I'm eating in a restaurant now.
I'm working now.
I'm watching TV right now.

I don't usually eat in restaurants.
I work every day.
I normally watch TV in the evenings.

Exercise 1

lose   *lost*
Continue.

give	marry	become	drive	spend
....	....	....	....	....

win	come	die	read	buy
....	....	....	....	....

begin	fall	take	write	meet
....	....	....	....	....

David and Elizabeth Kaufman got married exactly a year ago, so tonight they're eating in an expensive restaurant. They don't usually eat in expensive restaurants. They usually eat at home.

Look at this:

	Usual Dinner		Dinner Tonight	
	David	**Elizabeth**	**David**	**Elizabeth**
Appetizer	soup	soup	shrimp cocktail	melon
Entree	franks beans	franks beans	filet mignon	filet mignon
Dessert	yogurt and fruit	yogurt and fruit	apple pie with ice cream	chocolate cake with whipped cream
Drink	water	water	apple juice	apple juice

Exercise 2

Answer these questions.

Do they usually have soup?   *Yes, they do.*
Is David having soup tonight?   *No, he isn't.*

1. Does Elizabeth usually have melon? ....

2. Is Elizabeth having melon tonight? ....

3. Do they usually have franks and beans? ....

4. Are they having franks and beans tonight? ....

5. Does Elizabeth usually have water? ....

6. Is she having water tonight? ....

Exercise 3

David usually has water, but tonight he's having apple juice.
They usually have franks and beans, but tonight they're having filet mignon.

Write four sentences.

1. ....
....

2. ....
....

3. ....
....

4. ....
....

Exercise 4

They don't usually have filet mignon. They're having filet mignon tonight.
Elizabeth doesn't usually have melon. She's having melon tonight.

Write four sentences.

1. .... shrimp cocktail.

2. .... chocolate cake.

3. .... apple pie with ice cream.

4. .... apple juice.

Unit 55

Language Summary

I	was	doing the dishes.		Was	I	doing the dishes?		Yes,	I	was.
He	wasn't				he			No	he	wasn't.
She	was not				she				she	

We	were	doing the dishes.		Were	we	doing the dishes?		Yes,	we	were.
You	weren't				you			No,	you	weren't.
They	were not				they				they	

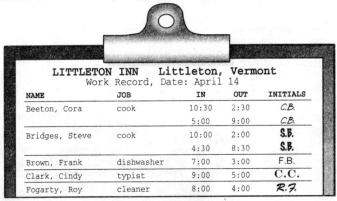

LITTLETON INN   Littleton, Vermont
Work Record, Date: April 14

NAME	JOB	IN	OUT	INITIALS
Beeton, Cora	cook	10:30	2:30	C.B.
		5:00	9:00	C.B.
Bridges, Steve	cook	10:00	2:00	S.B.
		4:30	8:30	S.B.
Brown, Frank	dishwasher	7:00	3:00	F.B.
Clark, Cindy	typist	9:00	5:00	C.C.
Fogarty, Roy	cleaner	8:00	4:00	R.F.

This is a page from the work record of the Littleton Inn.

Exercise 1

Frank Brown/8:00 AM
What was he doing at eight o'clock in the morning? He was washing dishes.   Continue.

1. Steve Bridges and Cora Beeton/ 12:30 PM

....

....

2. Cindy Clark/10:00 AM

....

....

3. Roy Fogarty/9:15 AM

....

....

Exercise 2

Was Frank Brown washing dishes at 3:30 in the afternoon? *No, he wasn't.*
Write answers.

1. Were Steve Bridges and Cora Beeton cooking at eleven o'clock in the morning?

....

2. Was Roy Fogarty cleaning at nine o'clock in the morning?

....

3. Was Cindy Clark typing at five-thirty in the afternoon?

....

Exercise 3

Where was Frank Brown working at eight o'clock? He was working in the kitchen.

1. .... Steve Bridges and Cora Beeton ....one o'clock?
.... in the kitchen.

2. .... Cindy Clark .... eleven o'clock?
.... in the office.

3. .... Roy Fogarty .... ten o'clock?
.... upstairs.

4. .... Roy Fogarty .... three o'clock?
.... downstairs.

Unit 56

Language Summary

He	was	walking to his car	when	somebody hit him.
		reading a book		it happened.

Look at this:

Present	Past	Present	Past	Present	Past
run	*ran*	*hit*	*hit*	*put*	*put*

Last year the *Albatross*, a Norwegian cruise ship, was crossing the Atlantic when it hit an iceberg. It was nine o'clock at night. Luckily, it wasn't a very big iceberg, but the passengers had a terrible shock. When the ship hit the iceberg, some of them were watching a movie in the ship's theater. The movie was *The Titanic*.

Look at this:

When the ship hit the iceberg at nine o'clock, the passengers were doing different things.

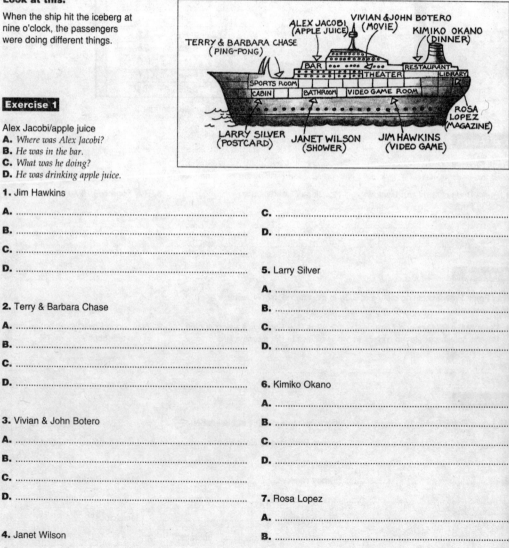

Exercise 1

Alex Jacobi/apple juice
A. *Where was Alex Jacobi?*
B. *He was in the bar.*
C. *What was he doing?*
D. *He was drinking apple juice.*

1. Jim Hawkins

A. ....

B. ....

C. ....

D. ....

2. Terry & Barbara Chase

A. ....

B. ....

C. ....

D. ....

3. Vivian & John Botero

A. ....

B. ....

C. ....

D. ....

4. Janet Wilson

A. ....

B. ....

C. ....

D. ....

5. Larry Silver

A. ....

B. ....

C. ....

D. ....

6. Kimiko Okano

A. ....

B. ....

C. ....

D. ....

7. Rosa Lopez

A. ....

B. ....

C. ....

D. ....

Jim Hawkins
jump/ocean

Janet Wilson
run/bathroom

Alex Jacobi
climb/lifeboat

Vivian & John Botero
leave/theater

When the ship hit the iceberg, Jim Hawkins was playing a video game.

A: *What did he do?*
B: *He jumped into the ocean.*

Write about the others.

1. Alex Jacobi

A: ....

B: ....

2. Janet Wilson

A: ....

B: ....

3. Vivian & John Botero

A: ....

B: ....

Exercise 3

Fill in the blanks.

Last week a Boeing 747, an American ...., was .... the Atlantic when it

flew into a storm. It was one o'clock in the afternoon. When it .... into the storm,

some of the .... were .... a movie. The .... was *The Great Airline Disaster*.

Exercise 4

When the plane flew into the storm, the passengers were
doing different things.

Patricia Chapman *was looking* out of the window.

Mr. & Mrs. Spencer were tired, and they *were sleeping*.

Fill in the blanks.

Ann & David Leung .... dinner.

Carlos Guzman .... a movie.

Joy Kovacs .... a book.

Suzy & Peter Vogel .... orange juice.

The pilot .... the plane.

Virginia Sanchez .... a letter.

Kate & Angela Martin .... to some friends.

The flight attendants .... people their meals.

Unit 57

Language Summary

I	could	drive	when	I	was	ten.	
He	couldn't	swim		he		eighteen.	
She	could not	play the piano		she		twenty.	
We							
You				we	were		
They				you			
				they			

Could	I	swim	when	I	was	ten?	Yes, I could.	
	he			he		eighteen?	No, I couldn't.	
	she			she		twenty?		
	we							
	you			we	were			
	they			you				
				they				

Tonight Amy Ching is playing in a concert with the
Bronx Symphony Orchestra. She's only ten years old.
She could play the piano when she was four. She
could also read music. She was a very clever child.
She could talk and walk when she was nine months
old. She could read and write when she was three,
and she could speak French when she was six.

Exercise 1

A: *Can she read music?*
B: *Yes, she can. She could read music when she was four.*

Now write four questions and four answers.

1. A: .... **B:** ....

2. A: .... **B:** ....

3. A: .... **B:** ....

4. A: .... **B:** ....

Exercise 2

A: *Could she read music when she was three?*
B: *No, she couldn't, but she could read music when she was four.*

Now write two questions and two answers.

1. A: ....

    B: ....

2. A: ....

    B: ....

Exercise 3

Answer these questions with *Yes, I could* or *No, I couldn't.*

1. Could you read when you were
three?

....

2. Could you write when you were
eight?

3. Could you speak English when you
were six?

....

4. Could you ride a bike when you
were four?

5. Could you walk when you were
two?

....

6. Could you talk when you were six
months old?

Unit 58

Language Summary

I You We They	have don't have	to	do this.	Do	I you we they	have	to	do this.	Yes, she does. No, she doesn't.	I You We They He She	can't can	do this.
He She	has doesn't have			Does	he she				Yes, you do. No, you don't.			

Exercise 1

You can't eat or drink here.

Write sentences.

1. ....
2. ....
3. ....
4. ....
5. ....

Exercise 2

You have to turn left.

Write sentences.

1. ....
2. ....
3. ....
4. ....
5. ....

Exercise 3

WHY GO AWAY?

See the U.S.A.!

You don't have to get a passport…
or a visa
or foreign money
or electrical adapters
or shots
or an international driver's license!

UNITED STATES TRAVEL BUREAU • WASHINGTON, DC

You don't have have to get a passport.

Write five sentences.

1. ....
2. ....
3. ....
4. ....
5. ....

Exercise 4

Answer these questions with *Yes, I do/No, I don't/Yes, I can/No, I can't.*

In your country:

1. Do you have to wear a uniform to school? ....
2. Can you drive without a license? ....
3. Do you have to carry an ID card? ....
4. Can you travel without a passport? ....
5. Do you have to pay taxes? ....
6. Do you have to take tests? ....
7. Do you have to pay the doctor? ....
8. Do you have to study? ....

Look at this:

Long distance calls

In many countries you don't have to call the operator when you want to make a long distance call. You can call direct. In many parts of the United States, to make a call to any point in the U.S.A., Puerto Rico, or Canada, you first press "1," then the area code, and then the local phone number. For example, to call 288-5547 in Chicago, press:

1	+	312	+	288-5547
Access Code		Area Code		Local Number

To call other parts of the world from the U.S.A., you press the international access code, then the country code, then the city code, and then the local number. For example, to call 532-9310 in Mexico City, press:

011	+	52	+	5	+	532-9310
International Access Code		Country Code	City Code			Local Number

You have to look in the phone book or call the operator for the codes. To call collect or person-to-person, the access code is "0" for calls in the U.S.A. and "01" for international calls.

To use your long distance calling card, you have to press "0," then the number you want to reach, including access code, country code, and city code or area code. You will hear a "beep." You then press your personal number (which appears on your card) and your call will be charged to your account.

Exercise 1

Make a conversation. Put the sentences into the correct order. Write 1–7 in the boxes.

☐ I'm sorry, but Bobby's out.

☐ Hello?

☐ Could I leave a message?

☐ Oh. When do you expect him back?

☐ Hello. Is Bobby Lang there?

☐ I'm not sure.

☐ Yes, of course.

Exercise 2

Look at the second conversation in the Student Book, and ask for a friend's number. Complete this conversation with your friend's name, address, and number.

A: Pacific Bell. What name and city?

B: ....

....

A: The number is ....

Exercise 3

Look at the third conversation in the Student Book.

You want to call a friend in Cali, Colombia. The country code is 57. You are in a hotel in Los Angeles.

A: Hotel operator.

B: ....

A: Yes. Press 9 for an external line. Then press 011.

B: OK. What next?

A: ....

B: OK. Cali's 3, I think.

A: ....

B: That's great. Thank you.

Exercise 4

Answer these questions.

1. Do you have a phone?...

2. What's your number?...

3. What's your area code?...

4. Can you dial direct to other cities in your country? ....

Other countries? ....

5. What's the country code for your country?.......................

Unit 60

Exercise 1

Fill in the blanks using verbs from the list.

was	*majored*
became	*lives*
graduated	*left*
is	*started*

Robert Mancini .... born on August 24, 1960, in Philadelphia. He .... from

high school in 1978. In 1979 he .... college in New York. He .... in medicine.

In 1988 he .... college and .... a doctor. His first job was at a hospital in

Philadelphia. He .... single and .... alone.

Exercise 2

Now write about Kelly Wong. Use these notes to help you.

<u>Personal details</u>
Name: Kelly Wong
Date of birth: 3/5/65
Place of birth: San Diego

<u>Education</u>
 High school — graduated 1983
College in Los Angeles — 1984–1988
Majored in Physics.

<u>Work</u>
1988 — became a teacher
First job — high school in San Diego

<u>Family</u>
Married. Has two children.

Kelly Wong was born on ....

....

....

....

....

....

....

....

....

....

Exercise 3

Now write a short paragraph about yourself.

....

....

....

....

....

....

Unit 61

Language Summary

I	've	opened it.	Have	I	opened it?			Yes, I have.
You	have	closed it.		you	closed it?			No, I haven't.
We	haven't	done it.		we	done it?			
They	have not			they				
He	's		Has	he				Yes, he has.
She	has			she				No, he hasn't.
It	hasn't			it				
	has not							

Look at this:

What's she going to do?　　What's she doing?　　What's she done?
She's going to wash it.　　She's washing it.　　She's washed it.

1. ....

He's going to open the window.

2. ....

He's ironing his clothes.

3. ....

She's made a call.

4. ....

What are they doing?

Unit 62

Language Summary

I	've	been	there.	Have	I	been there?	Yes,	I have.	Where	have	I	been?
You	have	gone			you			he has.			you	gone?
We	haven't				we						we	
They	have not				they		No,	I haven't.			they	
								he hasn't.				
He	's			Has	he					has	he	
She	has				she						she	
It	hasn't										it	
	has not											

Exercise 1

She has some bread. *She's been to the bakery.*
He has some new shoes. *He's been to the shoe store.*

1. He has some steak.

....

2. They have some money.

....

3. I have some stamps.

....

4. She has some aspirin.

....

5. She has a new book.

....

6. He has a new CD.

....

7. The children have new toys.

....

8. They're eating candy.

....

Exercise 2

They weren't here a minute ago. They're here now. *Where have they been?*

1. He wasn't here yesterday. He's here now.

....

2. Mark and Mary weren't here an hour ago. They're here now.

....

3. She wasn't here last week. She's here now.

....

4. The dog wasn't here a minute ago. It's here now.

....

Exercise 3

He was here. He isn't here now. *Where's he gone?*

1. They were here. They aren't here now.

....

2. Erica was at home. She isn't at home now.

....

3. Mr. and Mrs. Fernandez were in the living room. They aren't there now.

....

4. The cat was in the yard. It isn't there now.

....

Exercise 4

Ana has a toothache. She isn't here. *She's gone to the dentist.*

1. John needs some money. He isn't here.

....

2. Kelly broke her arm. She isn't here.

....

3. Paul needs some stamps. He isn't here.

....

4. Andrea forgot to get eggs. She isn't here.

....

Unit 63

I	've	just	done that.
You	have	already	painted that.
We			washed that.
They			
He/She/It	's has		

Look at this:

do—did—done
go—went—gone
am/is/are—was/were—been

open—opened—opened
close—closed—closed
call—called—called
study—studied—studied

Exercise 1

What does U.S. mean? It means United States.

Write questions and answers using: P.O., ESP, GOP, UFO, U.N., W.H.O. (You can use a dictionary.)

1. ....
2. ....
3. ....
4. ....
5. ....
6. ....

Exercise 2

What's she just done?
She's just washed the dog.

1. .... he
.... ?
.... the floor.

2. .... they
.... ?
.... a game.

3. .... sh
....
.... a doo

Exercise 3

Have you called a friend today? *Yes, I have* or *No, I haven't.*
Continue.

1. Have you combed your hair today?

   ....

2. Have you listened to the radio today?

   ....

3. Have you been shopping this week?

   ....

4. Have you visited a friend this week?

   ....

Exercise 4

Is she going to wash her hair? *No, she's already washed it.*

1. Is he going to brush his teeth?

   ....

2. Are they going to clean the house?

   ....

3. Is she going to do the dishes?

   ....

4. Are you going to finish your homework?

Language Summary

There	's is	too much	pollution. dirt.
	are 're	too many	people. problems.

There	isn't is not	enough	fresh air. water.
	aren't are not	enough	houses. jobs.

Look at this:

How many quarters?
How many dimes?   How much money?

How many apples?
How many pears?   How much fruit?

Exercise 1

Look at the examples and do the same with: gallons of gas/gas/loaves of bread/bread/cars/pollution/oil/smoke/bananas/food/minutes/time/hours/days/jobs/appointments/work/news/music/information/excitement/dirt/rice/water/people/books/houses/apartments/milk/glasses.

How much?   *money/fruit*   ....

....

....

How many?   *dimes/quarters/apples/pears* ....

....

....

Exercise 2

Big cities have a lot of problems. Look at the words in the list and write ten sentences. Begin with:

There isn't enough ... / There aren't enough ...
There's too much ... / There are too many ...

apartments/parks/work for young people/police officers/
fresh air/pollution/cars/people/office buildings/traffic/noise

There aren't enough apartments.

1. ....
2. ....
3. ....
4. ....
5. ....
6. ....
7. ....
8. ....
9. ....
10. ....

Language Summary

I	've	been to Washington.
You	have	seen the Capitol.
We		
They		
He	's	
She	has	
It		

I	haven't	been to Washington	yet.
You	have not	seen the Capitol	
We			
They			
He	hasn't		
She	has not		
It			

Yes,	I	have.
	he	has.
No,	I	haven't.
	he	hasn't.

I've	never	been to Washington before.
He's		seen the Capitol.

Have you	ever	been to Washington?
Has he		seen the Capitol?

TRACY CHAMPION:
TOUR OF LATIN AMERICA

ITINERARY: JUNE 1-9	DAY 5: LIMA
DAY 1: MEXICO CITY	DAY 6: SANTIAGO
DAY 2: PANAMA CITY	DAY 7: SÃO PAULO
DAY 3: BOGOTA	DAY 8: RIO DE JANEIRO
DAY 4: GUAYAQUIL	DAY 9: CARACAS

Tracy Champion, the famous singer, is on a concert tour of Latin America. It's the fifth day of the tour, and she's in Lima.

TECHNOCRAT:
TOUR OF THE UNITED STATES

ITINERARY: JUNE 1-9	DAY 5: MIAMI
DAY 1: BOSTON	DAY 6: NEW ORLEANS
DAY 2: NEW YORK	DAY 7: DALLAS
DAY 3: WASHINGTON	DAY 8: SAN FRANCISCO
DAY 4: ATLANTA	DAY 9: LOS ANGELES

Technocrat is a very popular group. They're on a concert tour of the United States. It's the fifth day of the tour, and they're in Miami.

Exercise 1

She's been to Mexico City.
She hasn't been to São Paulo yet.

Write six sentences.

1. ....
2. ....
3. ....
4. ....
5. ....
6. ....

Exercise 2

They've been to Boston.
They haven't been to Dallas yet.

Write six sentences.

1. ....
2. ....
4. ....
5. ....

Has she been to Mexico City yet? Yes, she has.
Has she been to São Paulo yet? No, she hasn't.

Write six questions and answers.

1. ....   4. ....
2. ....   5. ....
3. ....   6. ....

Have they been to Boston yet? Yes, they have.
Have they been to Dallas yet? No, they haven't.

Write six questions and answers.

1. ....   4. ....
2. ....   5. ....
3. ....   6. ....

Mount Fuji   *Have you ever seen Mount Fuji?*

Write eight questions. Answer them with
Yes, I have or *No, I haven't.*

the Empire State Building	an elephant
a Rolls-Royce car	the Space Shuttle
a Superman movie	the Taj Mahal
the San Francisco Ballet	a professional baseball game

1. ....
2. ....
3. ....
4. ....
5. ....
6. ....
7. ....
8. ....

He/Japan/Mount Fuji.
He's been to Japan, and he's seen Mount Fuji.

1. She/Rome/the Colosseum ....
....

2. They/London/Buckingham Palace ....
....

3. She/Athens/the Acropolis...........................
....

4. He/Mexico/the Aztec pyramids ....
....

5. I/San Francisco/the Golden Gate Bridge.......................
....

6. We/Honolulu/Waikiki Beach..............................

Unit 66

Language Summary

How	much	have you	done?
	many	has he	

am/is/are	was/were	been
go	went	gone
see	saw	seen
take	took	taken
send	sent	sent
spend	spent	spent
buy	bought	bought
meet	met	met

	Pat Kelly is from San Francisco. He's on vacation, and he's touring Japan.	Mr. and Mrs. Vincent are American. They're on vacation in Italy.	Trudy Markham is from Canada. She's on vacation in Colombia.
Places visited	Tokyo Kyoto	Rome Naples	Cartagena Bogotá
Going to visit	Osaka Hiroshima	Florence Bologna	Cali Medellín
Places seen	the Meiji Shrine the Temple of the Golden Pavilion	the Colosseum the isle of Capri	a lot of Spanish forts the Gold Museum
Things bought	some souvenirs	some pictures	2 wool ponchos
Money spent	$1,500	$1,200	$800
People met	not many	a few	a lot
Postcards	ten	twenty	fifteen
Photographs	0	a lot	about 60

Exercise 1

Look at this postcard. Pat Kelly is in Japan. He's sending a postcard home.

POSTCARD

PLACE STAMP HERE

Dear Mom and Dad,
   Well, I've been to Tokyo and Kyoto. I haven't been to Hiroshima yet. I've seen the Meiji Shrine and the Temple of the Golden Pavilion. I've bought some souvenirs. It's expensive here. I've spent $1,500. I haven't met many people. I've sent 10 postcards to my friends. I haven't taken any photographs. That's all for now.   Love, Pat

Mr. & Mrs. P.J. Kelly
756 Cortland Ave.
San Francisco, CA
94110
U.S.A.

Now write a postcard for Mr. and Mrs. Vincent, beginning: We've...

POSTCARD

PLACE STAMP HERE

Dear Michelle,
....
....
....
....
....
....
....
....
....
....
....

Ms. Michelle Wallace
2538 Laurence Blvd.
Miami, FL 33102
U.S.A.

Exercise 2

Now write about Trudy's vacation. She's in Colombia.

She's been to ....
....
....
....

Unit 67

Language Summary

Have	I you we they	ever	done that? drunk this? seen it? eaten this? bought that?
Has	she he		

Yes,	I he	have. has.
No,	I he	haven't. hasn't.

When	did	I you we they he she	do that? drink it? see it? eat it? buy that?

Look at this:

drink—drank—drunk
eat—ate—eaten
drive—drove—driven
break—broke—broken

have—had—had
find—found—found
lose—lost—lost
hit—hit—hit

Exercise 1

Now complete this.

meet ....   do ....   go ....

send ....   see ....   take ....

Exercise 2

Look at the example. Complete the conversations.

Example:

A: Have you ever *seen* an elephant?
B: Yes, I have.
A: Where did you *see* it?
B: I *saw* it at the zoo.

1. A: Have they ever met a movie star?
B: Yes, they have.
A: Who did they .... ?
B: They .... Tom Cruise.

2. A: Have you ever .... anybody?
B: Yes, I have.
A: Oh, who did you hit?
B: I .... my brother!

3. A: Have you ever .... in the hospital?
B: Yes, I have.
A: Why .... you in the hospital?
B: Because I .... very sick.

4. A: Has he ever .... a Corvette?
B: Yes, he has.
A: Really? When did he .... it?
B: He .... it last year.

5. A: Has she ever .... champagne?
B: Yes, she has.
A: Oh, where did she .... it?
B: She .... some at her sister's wedding.

6. A: Have you ever .... any money?
B: Yes, I have.
A: How much did you .... ?
B: I lost $20.

7. A: Have you ever found anything in the street?
B: Yes, I have.
A: What did you .... ?
B: I .... a pocketbook.

8. A: Has he ever .... Japanese food?
B: Yes, he has.
A: Where did he eat it?
B: He .... it in San Francisco.

9. A: Have you ever taken a driving test?
B: Yes, I have.
A: When did you .... it?
B: I .... it in 1991.

10. A: Have you ever .... to a famous person?
B: Yes, we have.
A: Oh, who did you .... to?
B: We spoke to Madonna.

11. A: Has she ever .... your house?
B: Yes, she has.
A: When did she visit you?
B: She .... us last week.

Unit 68

Look at this:

long ... longer	big ... bigger	dry ... drier	large ... larger	good ... better
short ... shorter	wet ... wetter	heavy ... heavier	nice ... nicer	bad ... worse
old ... older	thin ... thinner			

−		+
less expensive	expensive	more expensive
less comfortable	comfortable	more comfortable
less economical	economical	more economical

Exercise 1

young *younger* Continue.

1. nice	**4.** bad	**7.** near	**10.** lucky	**13.** near	**16.** dirty
....	....	....	....	....	....
2. sunny	**5.** hot	**8.** white	**11.** good	**14.** noisy	**17.** warm
....	....	....	....	....	....
3. dark	**6.** fresh	**9.** cheap	**12.** sad	**15.** quiet	**18.** long
....	....	....	....	....	....

Exercise 2

less interesting interesting *more interesting*   Continue.

1. .... exciting ....
2. .... important ....
3. .... dangerous ....
4. .... comfortable ....
5. .... expensive ....
6. .... economical ....

Exercise 3

Sporttini/fast
The Sporttini is faster than the Hudson.

Hudson/economical
The Sporttini is less economical than the Hudson.

Hudson/exciting
The Hudson is less exciting than the Sporttini.

1. Hudson/slow ....
....

2. Sporttini/expensive ....
....

3. Hudson/heavy ....
....

4. Sporttini/small ....
....

5. Sporttini/comfortable ....
....

6. Sporttini/short ....
....

7. Hudson/long ....
....

8. Sporttini/light ....
....

9. Hudson/dangerous ....
....

10. Hudson/big ....
....

Language Summary

I	have to	see it.		Do	I	have to see it?		Yes, I do.
You	don't have to			Did	you			No, I don't.
We					we			
They	had to				they			Yes, I did.
	didn't have to			Does	he			No, I didn't.
He	has to			Did	she			
She	doesn't have to							
	had to							
	didn't have to							

Bubba Carruthers is a player for the Red Bay Canners. The Canners are one of the teams of the Continental Football League. The football season begins in September and ends in January. In the summer the players have to train hard. The coach gives them a lot of rules.

Exercise 1

get up/6 o'clock   *They have to get up at six o'clock.*

Continue.

1. go to bed/10 o'clock ....

....

2. practice/3 hours a day ....

....

3. run/2 miles/every day ....

....

4. eat/steak and salad/lunch ....

....

5. stay in/hotel/before a game ....

Exercise 2

Bubba is on vacation in the spring.

He doesn't have to get up at six o'clock.

Look at Exercise 1, and write five sentences.

1. ....

....

2. ....

....

3. ....

....

4. ....

....

5. ....

....

Exercise 3

Bart Barr is the coach of the Red Bay Canners. Ten years ago he was a football player, too. The rules were the same ten years ago.

He had to get up at six o'clock.

Look at Exercise 1, and write five sentences.

1. ....

....

2. ....

....

3. ....

....

4. ....

....

5. ....

....

Exercise 4

He also had his vacation in the spring.

He didn't have to get up at six o'clock.

Look at Exercise 1, and write five sentences.

1. ....

....

2. ....

....

3. ....

....

4. ....

....

5. ....

....

Unit 70

Language Summary

long ... longer ... the longest
short ... shorter ... the shortest
old ... older ... the oldest

big ... bigger ... the biggest
wet ... wetter ... the wettest
thin ... thinner ... the thinnest

large ... larger ... the largest
nice ... nicer ... the nicest

dry ... drier ... the driest
heavy ... heavier ... the heaviest

good ... better ... the best
bad ... worse ... the worst

– ◄───► +

| the least expensive | less expensive | expensive | more expensive | the most expensive |
| the least comfortable | less comfortable | comfortable | more comfortable | the most comfortable |

Exercise 1

young: **A.** *younger* **B.** *the youngest* Continue.

1. noisy: **A.** .... **B.** ....
2. white: **A.** .... **B.** ....
3. hot: **A.** .... **B.** ....
4. good: **A.** .... **B.** ....
5. sad: **A.** .... **B.** ....
6. lucky: **A.** .... **B.** ....
7. big: **A.** .... **B.** ....
8. bad: **A.** .... **B.** ....
9. light: **A.** .... **B.** ....
10. high: **A.** .... **B.** ....

Exercise 2

Continue.

A. *the least interesting*
B. *less interesting*
C. *interesting*
D. *more interesting*
E. *the most interesting*

1. A. ....
B. ....
C. important
D. ....
E. ....

2. A. ....
B. ....
C. exciting
D. ....
E. ....

3. A. ....
B. ....
C. dangerous
D. ....
E. ....

Exercise 3

A/B/interesting

House A is more interesting than house B.

1. C/B modern ....
2. A/C expensive ....
3. B/C beautiful ....

Exercise 4

A/expensive

House A is the most expensive.

1. A/modern ....
2. B/beautiful ....
3. A/interesting ....

Exercise 5

C/interesting

House C is the least interesting.

1. C/expensive ....
2. B/modern ....
3. C/beautiful ....

Guide to New Motorcycles
This week: 3 Motorcycles (1000cc and over)

	Kawaskari 1100 cc	Handley Davidson 1200 cc	BMV 1000 cc
TOP SPEED (miles per hour) and acceleration	165 m.p.h. (0 to 60 in 4 seconds)	95 m.p.h. (0 to 60 in 6 seconds)	125 m.p.h. (0 to 60 in 6 seconds)
ECONOMY (miles per gallon)	29 city 43 highway	30 city 45 highway	28 city 40 highway
COMFORT very comfortable ★★★★★ very uncomfortable ★	★★★	★★★★★	★★★★
NOISE very quiet ★★★★★ very noisy ★	★★★	★★	★
WEIGHT	500 lb	600 lb	550 lb
LENGTH	6 feet 6 inches	7 feet 2 inches	6 feet 11 inches
PRICE	$9,795	$11,995	$10,495

Exercise 6

The Kawaskari is faster than the BMV, and the BMV is faster than the Handley Davidson.

Write sentences using these words: economical/ noisy/long/heavy/expensive/comfortable.

1. ....
....
2. ....
....
3. ....
....
4. ....
....
5. ....
....
6. ....
....

Exercise 7

Which is fastest?
The Kawaskari is the fastest.

Write questions and answers.

1. ....
....
2. ....
....
3. ....
....
4. ....
....
5. ....
....
6. ....
....

Unit 71

Language Summary

The CN Tower's very tall.
It's taller than the Eiffel Tower in Paris.
It's the tallest tower in the world.

Look at this:

take—took—taken
buy—bought—bought

Exercise 1

take   *took*   *taken*

Continue.

do	....	....	go	....	....	get	....	....
drive	....	....	feel	....	....	send	....	....
hit	....	....	see	....	....	find	....	....
break	....	....	drink	....	....	lose	....	....
eat	....	....	meet	....	....	spend	....	....

Exercise 2

This car is fast! (drive)

It's the fastest car I've ever driven.

1. This book's interesting! (read)

....

2. This pizza is delicious! (eat)

....

3. This city is exciting! (visit)

....

4. This coffee's good! (drink)

....

5. This language is difficult! (study)

....

6. This wedding is big! (go to)

....

7. She is a famous movie star! (meet)

....

8. This question is difficult! (answer)

....

Exercise 3

The CN Tower/tall building
The CN Tower's the tallest building in the world.

1. The cheetah/fast animal

....

2. Rolls-Royce/comfortable car

....

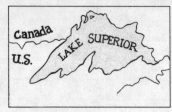

3. Lake Superior/large lake

....

4. Antarctica/cold place

....

Unit 72

Language Summary

Offers
I'll open the window.

Requests
Will you open the window?
Of course, I will.
No, I won't.

Suggestions
Let's go to the movies.
Why don't we go to the theater?

Exercise 1

Bruce is a hairdresser. He has a new assistant today. He's asking her to help him.

 some shampoo
Will you bring me some shampoo?

2. the scissors
....
....

4. a mirror
....
....

 1. a hair dryer
....
....

3. a towel
....
....

5. a comb
....
....

Exercise 2

A: The phone's ringing. **B:** *I'll answer it!* Continue.

1. A: I'm hot and the window's closed!
   B: ....

3. A: I have a headache.
   B: ....

5. A: I'm very cold. The door's open.
   B: ....

2. A: My suitcase is very heavy.
   B: ....

4. A: I don't have any money.
   B: ....

6. A: I'm thirsty.
   B: ....

Exercise 3

Can you fix it now? (later) *No, I'll fix it later.* Continue.

1. Can he do it today? (tomorrow)
....

3. Can she ask him now? (soon)
....

2. Can they help me now? (in a minute)
....

4. Can you get it today? (next week)
....

Exercise 4

A: *Why don't we go to the movies?*
B: *No, let's go to the theater to see* Hamlet.
Write three more conversations.

1. A: ....
   B: ....

2. A: ....
   B: ....
   ....

3. A: ....
   B: ....

Unit 73

Language Summary

| This car isn't | as | fast | as | that car. |
| | | comfortable | | |

| It's | as | cold | as | ice. |
| | | black | | night. |

It's	the	most interesting	movie	I've	ever	seen.
		best/worst	play	she's		been to.
		most exciting				

| It's | the same as | yours/ours/theirs. |
| They're | different from | mine/his/hers. |

Exercise 1

Look at the first conversation in the Student Book. Complete this conversation.

A: I like your room!

B: ....

A: No, it isn't. ....

B: Is it?

A: .... more comfortable.

Exercise 2

A: I don't have any money. **B:** *Why don't you go to the bank?*

1. A: I have a toothache.

   B: ....

2. A: I'm sick.

   B: ....

3. A: I need some bread.

   B: ....

4. A: I'm hungry.

   B: ....

Exercise 3

Fords/fast/Ferraris   *Fords aren't as fast as Ferraris.*

1. Mount McKinley/high/Mount Everest

....

2. BIC pens/expensive/Parker pens

....

3. English/boring/math

....

4. cats/dangerous/dogs

....

5. Italy/hot/Saudi Arabia

....

6. English/difficult/Japanese

....

Exercise 4

He has a Rabbit convertible. I have a Rabbit convertible.   *His car is the same as mine.*

1. They have a Ford. We have a Ford.

....

2. She has an Omega watch. I have an Omega watch.

....

3. He has a Parker pen. She has a Parker pen.

....

4. We have a Sony TV. They have a Sony TV.

....

Exercise 5

I drove a Cadillac. It's a good car.   *It's the best car I've ever driven.*

1. I saw *Escape From Earth*. It's a good movie.

....

2. She saw *Frankenstein Alive!* It's a bad movie.

....

3. We heard Technocrat. They're a good band.

....

4. He read *The Godfather*. It's an interesting book.

....

5. I took some photos. They're very good photos.

....

Unit 74

Language Summary

	some	any?	no	not ... any	every
Thing	something	anything?	nothing	not ... anything	everything
Person	somebody	anybody?	nobody	not ... anybody	everybody
	someone	anyone?	no one	not ... anyone	everyone
Place	somewhere	anywhere?	nowhere	not ... anywhere	everywhere

Exercise 1

I want some seats. *Are there any left?*
I want some coffee. *Is there any left?*
Continue.

1. I want some tickets.

....

2. I want some soup.

....

3. I want some doughnuts.

....

4. I want some milk.

....

5. I want some bread.

....

Exercise 2

seats *There are no seats left.*

sugar *There's no sugar left.*

1. bread

....

2. doughnuts

....

3. tickets

....

4. soup

....

Exercise 3

Complete this conversation.
Use these words:
anything/something/nothing/everything.

Mr. Jenson is in a store.

A: I'm looking for .... for my son. It's his birthday next week. .... is so expensive. Have you got .... cheaper?

B: I'm sorry sir. .... 's cheap nowadays.

Exercise 4

Complete this conversation.
Use these words:
nobody/somebody/everybody/anybody.

A: I went to Clint and Anita's wedding last Saturday. .... from the office was there—even the boss.

B: Oh, I love weddings. Did .... cry?

A: No, ... cried.

B: What about the reception?

A: Oh, it was very funny. .... danced on the table.

B: Who was it?

A: I don't know.

Exercise 5

Complete this conversation.
Use these words:
everywhere/nowhere/somewhere/anywhere.

A: Let's go .... romantic tonight, Penny.

B: Do you have .... special in mind, Wayne?

A: No, ... in particular.

B: .... is romantic with you.

A: How about a burger and fries at MacGregor's?

B: Terrific!

Unit 75

Language Summary

I	've	been	here	for	two days.	How long	have you	been	here?
You	have				a few minutes.		has she		there?
We					six months.				
They					ten years.				
He	's			since	two o'clock.				
She	has				Tuesday.				
It					February.				

Exercise 1

I/1992   *I've been here since 1992.*

She/two days   *She's been here for two days.*   Continue.

1. We/Christmas...

2. They/four days ....

3. He/last weekend ....

4. I/ten years...

5. He/a few days ....

6. It/Saturday ....

7. She/six years ....

8. You/1991 ....

9. She/March 20 ....

10. It/ten minutes..

11. They/August ....

12. We/two hours..

Look at this: David Vargas and Pat Burnett went to college together. They finished in 1985.

Exercise 2

David Vargas became a businessman eight years ago. He bought a house four years ago and a Chevrolet at the same time.
Answer these questions.

1. When did he become a businessman?

....

2. When did he buy his house?

....

3. What about his car?

....

4. How long has he been a businessman?

....

5. How long has he had the house?

....

6. How long has he had his car?

....

Exercise 3

Pat Burnett became a rock star in 1987. In 1992 she retired to Palm Beach. She bought an apartment, a Ferrari, and a boat. She still has them. She hasn't worked since 1992.
Answer these questions.

1. When did she become a rock star?

....

2. When did she retire?

....

3. Where did she go?

....

4. How long has she had the apartment?

....

5. How long has she had the car and boat?

....

6. Has she worked since 1992?

....

Unit 76

Language Summary

You can't use it	during	the flight.		I'm afraid	you can't use the computer.
He was using it		the movie.		I'm sorry, but	we don't have any magazines.

Exercise 1

Fill in the blanks in this story.

Use these words: parked/opened/third/miles/rented/two/put/weren't/finished/saw/wearing/got in/driving/fourth/
come back/wasn't/wrong/waiting/carrying/stop/same/holding/got off/took/started.

It's three o'clock. Mr. Jackson has just .... a white Dodge on the
.... floor of a parking garage. It isn't his car. He .... it
yesterday. Mr. Jackson is in St. Louis on business. He's .... a dark
business suit, and he's .... a briefcase.

It's .... hours later. Mr. Jackson has .... his business,
and he has .... to the parking garage. He's .... for the
elevator. He's .... the car keys.

Mr. Jackson was very tired. The elevator didn't .... on the third floor.
It stopped on the .... floor. Mr. Jackson .... the elevator.
He .... a white Dodge in front of him. He walked over and
.... the key in the door. He .... the door, ...,
and .... the engine.

An hour later Mr. Jackson was forty .... from St. Louis. He was
.... along the highway when a police car stopped him. The police
officers .... very friendly. It .... Mr. Jackson's car. It was
the .... Dodge, but the keys were the .... They
.... him to the police station.

Exercise 2

What did Mr. Jackson say to the police officers?

....

....

Unit 77

Language Summary

One	of them	is happy.
		plays the piano.
Both	of them	are happy.
Neither		play the piano.
Some		
All		
None		

Exercise 1

One of them is tall.
Both of them are wearing watches.
Neither of them are wearing coats.

Write nine sentences.

Use these words: short/jackets/young/ties/old/baseball cap/
sneakers/jeans/T-shirts.

1. ....

2. ....   6. ....

3. ....   7. ....

4. ....   8. ....

5. ....   9. ....

Here is some information about six people.

Name	Languages	Sports	Likes
Makoto	French, Spanish, Japanese	Tennis, basketball, football	Sports, languages, cooking, television
Carrie	French, Spanish	Tennis, basketball, hockey	Sports, languages, rock music
Jasmine	French, Spanish, Japanese, German	Tennis, basketball, golf	Sports, languages, television, movies
Darren	French, Spanish, Arabic	Tennis, basketball, football, baseball	Sports, languages, rock music
Wendy	French, Spanish, German	Tennis, basketball	Sports, languages, ballet
Rafael	French, Spanish, German, Japanese, Chinese	Tennis, basketball, football, baseball	Sports, languages, cooking

Exercise 2

All of them speak French.

Write sentences using: all/some/none/one.

1. .... Spanish.   9. .... volleyball.

2. .... baseball.   10. .... cooking.

3. .... opera.   11. .... basketball.

4. .... Chinese.   12. .... golf.

5. .... Arabic.   13. .... languages.

6. .... rock music.   14. .... tennis.

7. .... ballet.   15. .... movies.

8. .... French.   16. .... television.

Unit 78

Look at this:

beat—beat—beaten   throw—threw—thrown
steal—stole—stolen   read—read—read

Exercise

Look at the newspaper. Look at Unit 78 in the Student Book.

Fill in the blanks.

THE WEEKLY GAZETTE

Wednesday, June 2   Marion, North Carolina   75¢

Sensational Bank Robbery
Second National Bank – $400,000 Stolen

.... bank robbery .... Marion last Friday. The robbers .... a smoke bomb .... the door of the Second National Bank and .... $300,000 in cash, and money orders .... $100,000.

Mr. Robert Gibson, president of the bank, ... in his office when .... The police .... six suspects. The thieves .... in a .... Ford Taurus. The police .... yet.

Mont Blanc Expedition Fails

Two women from Marion, part of a team of .... in the Alps, ... to reach .... Mont Blanc yesterday, but they .... because the weather .... bad. They .... postpone the climb .... next Monday. The weather .... worst .... 1992.

Sheep Missing!

Farmer Jim Munroe .... about a series of attacks .... animals. Something .... and .... seven sheep on his farm this year. .... bears up in the Blue Ridge Mountains, but .... a bear near Munroe's farm .... 30 years. The police said, "............... a large dog. Nobody .... the attacks." Mr. Munroe .... with a shotgun.

Have you seen this boy?

Tim Cook, 15 ...., of 243 Oak St., Marion, ... home .... month and nobody .... since, Tim's ...., Bruce Cook, ... police last week.

He .... a blue shirt, black shoes, and a .... He .... black .... and .... eyes. Please .... 461-4600 with ....

Exercise 1

You work in a florist shop. You are **A**.
Complete this conversation.

A: ....

B: Yes, I want to send some flowers to my wife in the hospital.

A: ....
....?

B: Well, what do you recommend?

A: ....
....

B: Fine. Half a dozen tulips, please.

A: ....?

B: Yes. "Get well soon. Love, Ed."

Exercise 2

Someone is giving a present to you. You are **B**.
Complete this conversation.

A: Hi! Here's a present for you.

B: ....? ....!
....?

A: Yes, go ahead.

B: ....
....
....

A: Thank *you*. You've been very kind to me.

Exercise 3

You are leaving a party. You have to catch the last bus home.
Complete this conversation.

A: ....
....

B: Oh, don't go now! The party's just starting.

A: ....

B: Oh, don't be silly. I'll give you a ride.

A: ....

B: Oh. Well, thanks for coming, and thanks for the lovely present.

Exercise 4

Now answer these questions.

1. Have you ever sent flowers to anyone?

....

2. Why did you send them?

....

3. When was your last birthday?

....

4. Did anyone send you a present for your birthday?

....

5. What was it?

....

Unit 80

Exercise 1

write — wrote — written

Fill in the blanks.

1. steal ....

2. .... threw ....

3. .... read

4. .... gotten

5. .... were ....

6. .... beaten

7. buy ....

8. .... hit

9. break ....

10. .... spent ....

Exercise 2

Fill in the blanks.

I	me	my
you	....	your
....	him	his
she	her	....
we	....	our
they	them	....

Exercise 3

What are they doing?

They're writing.

1. ....

2. ....

3. ....

Exercise 4

Write the opposites.

big *small*

1. difficult ....

2. cheap ....

3. tall ....

4. dangerous ....

Exercise 5

Write the adverbs.

slow *slowly*

1. good ....

2. bad ....

3. careful ....

4. quick ....

Exercise 6

Write *a*, *an*, or *some*.

an apple

1. .... book

2. .... sugar

3. .... milk

4. .... orange

Review

Read Units 41–80 in the Student Book and answer these questions.

Unit

41. What day of the week was December 26?

....

43. Where were Joe's children?

....

44. What did Phil eat on his trip?

....

45. What did Ron get at the bakery?

....

46. Who signed the letters?

....

47. How many times did the sheriff fire?

....

48. What did Paulo buy?

....

49. What happened after four weeks?

....

50. Who lost his shoe?

....

52. Who are the Virginia police looking for?

....

53. When did Jan become a paramedic?

....

54. What is Harriet's husband doing?

....

55. Where was the dog sitting?

....

56. What was the attacker wearing?

....

57. What could Josh do when he was 3?

....

58. Does Carmen have to stay in her room?

....

59. What's the area code for San Diego?

....

61. Who is Phil speaking to?

....

62. Where has Pete been?

....

63. Where is his pen?

....

64. Where was Gina born?

....

65. Where was Elmer yesterday?

....

66. Who has Elmer met?

....

67. When did she have the flu?

....

68. What can Dr. Finkel's new machine do?

....

69. Why did Jerry's grandfather have to go to the hospital?

....

70. Which is the biggest country in the world?

....

71. How far is Niagara Falls from the CN Tower?

....

72. What is in the cafeteria?

....

74. Are there any seats left for Tuesday night?

....

75. How long have Gina and Charlie lived in Arizona?

....

76. What can't Mr. Gabriel use during the flight?

....

77. Where are the Dixie Chickens from?

....

78. Where are the three climbers from?

....

79. How many roses did she buy?

....